MW01295136

Bena Blake Dillman

Patchwork Pieces Of Life

by
Rena Blake Dillman

"A Compilation of Short Stories that Will
Warm Your Heart and
Touch Your Spirit"

David Webster – Family Connections

Foreward by Anthony E. Carson

authorHOUSE™

1663 LIBERTY DRIVE, SUITE 200
BLOOMINGTON, INDIANA 47403
(800) 839-8640
WWW.AUTHORHOUSE.COM

First published by AuthorHouse 11/03/05

ISBN: 1-4208-7922-7 (sc)

Printed in the United States of America
Bloomington, Indiana

This book is printed on acid-free paper.

All scripture references are taken from the King James Version of the
Bible.

The quilt featured on the book cover was made by my
great-grandmother, Sally Turner Woods, in the early 1920's.
It was given to me as a wedding gift in 1962.

Rena may be reached at _patchworks@thedillmans.com_ or
Post Office Box 1980, Hope, Indiana 47246

Table of Contents

Dedication
Acknowledgements
Special Thanks
Foreward
Introduction

SECTION I – Memories, like old friends, …

Short Story

SECTION II – What happened to that young girl?

Short Story

SECTION VII – Where is that Grandmother?

Short Story

Conclusion

This book is dedicated to
My Grandmother -
Cora Turner Riley Snoddy

Thank you Grandma Cora for inspiring me to write this book by sharing your life stories. I treasure every moment we have spent together and love and admire you so very much.

Your oldest grandchild – Rena

Acknowledgements

First of all, glory to God for all He has done for me!

To my parents, Clifton and Nola Blake, thank you for loving each other as well as loving each of your children unconditionally.

Thank you Roger, Darrell, Ronald, Gregory, Robert and Randy for being my cohorts in childhood antics and my best buddies. I forgive you for all the BB shots to my legs and the times you tried to drown me. The motorcycle and Corvette rides more than made up for it.

A very special thanks to my husband, Don, who has encouraged me to be all that I want to be. My love always.

To our sons, Darrell and Jon, thank you for the privilege of being your Mom. You have brought love, joy, laughter and many gray hairs to my life.

Thank you Dana, for loving our son Darrell and giving us the most beautiful and gifted grandchildren on the planet.

To our grandchildren, Blake and Jessica, thank you for making our golden years truly "golden."

My parents Clifton and Nola Blake
with me at 2 months of age

Special Thanks

These true-life stories have been written over a period of several years as a legacy to my children and grandchildren. Many of them have been shared with family and friends, who often have encouraged me to include them in a book. A heart-stirring sermon by my pastor, Reverend Dan Mitchell, inspired me to complete this adventure. In his sermon he admonished our congregation, "Do not take your book, poem, song or masterpiece painting to your grave with you." I took his words to heart and began the process of putting this book together with the help of these very special people that God sent my way. Heath Harrison, David Webster and Pamela J. Anderson have invested hours of their time editing and have given support each step of the way. I offer my gratitude and thanks to them as well as the following who have also been my encouragers and prayer partners:

Rev. Tony and Martha Carson
Rev. Herman and Katie Stewart
David and Lisa Webster
Heath and Alicia Harrison
Shirley Ernest
Alice Lange
Ron Blake
Dave Oltman
Sue Randolph
Debbie Hatton
Jackie Hornaday
Margaret Ray
Vickie Phillips
Edna Bergman
Rosemary Moffett

Foreward

The year was 1983. My wife and I had walked into a pawnshop in the little Southern Indiana town of Hope to look for some snow skis. As we browsed around the store, we were drawn to an area with the most beautiful artwork hanging from the walls. While trying to determine the artist, we noticed that the only signature was a small feathery "R" in the bottom right-hand corner. Suddenly from somewhere behind us came this gentle voice, as soft as the signature on her paintings, saying, "May I help you?" Thus began a friendship that has lasted over twenty years.

A few months after that initial meeting, which must have been ordained of God, we had the privilege of baptizing Rena Dillman in the wonderful name of Jesus. For the next three years, she attended the church that I pastored in North Vernon, Indiana. However, Rena was more than just a member of our church. She became our art teacher, our prayer partner, our encourager, and most of all, our friend.

In 1987 I resigned as pastor of the church, and my family and I left Indiana for a new field of ministry. Over the next seventeen years, the friendship forged between the Dillmans and the Carsons only grew stronger.

It is with honor that I write the forward to her first book. Slip into something cozy and settle down in your most comfortable easy chair. For when you begin reading this book, you will not want to lay it down. Each page and chapter is from the heart of an artist. Each heart-warming story will paint a picture as vivid and realistic as those paintings we saw hanging on the wall of that old pawnshop so many years ago. And, each one will become a unique piece of patchwork in the memory quilt of life...the life of a wonderful Christian woman-Rena Dillman.

Anthony E. Carson

Introduction

My journey of faith began long before I was born. I have a rich heritage in faith as well as fear. Several generations of Godly grandmothers have passed on their unwavering faith in God to the next generation. From personal experiences I understand the scripture that speaks of the power of life and death being in the tongue. For many years, I spoke certain words because they had been repeatedly spoken to me. I did not realize their power, not until I came to the realization that I had more fear in my life than faith. I always thought of myself as a person of strong faith. However, through the years, fear has taken over at times causing weakness in my faith.

While writing my life stories, I have been able to travel through my memories and look again at the events of my life that have become landmarks of family faith. I can still recall the gripping and overwhelming fear at times during a family crisis. In addition, I can remember the protective bubble of my Heavenly Father who has never left my side. He has kept me from falling into that dark abyss of depression at times, especially after the death of my mother. Through His written and spoken word, He has poured faith into my vessel lifting me up out of the destructive clutches of fear. Many years ago, while I was going through a personal battle, my pastor provided a verse of scripture to encourage me. II Timothy 1: 7 states, "For God has not given us a spirit of fear, but of love, power and a sound mind." This verse of scripture has been my anthem when the spirit of fear has tried to force its icy fingers around my heart. It is my prayer these words will minister and lift you out of the trenches of fear in your life's journey and that faith and hope will rise up within you. Let it be so. AMEN!

SECTION I

Memories, like old friends, come to visit and sit a spell. Some linger, bringing a smile or a tear. Others rush in, and then quickly leave, never to return again.

His Angels Have Charge Over Us

I had no idea my grandmother had gone through such trying times as a small child. So typical of my grandmother was her loving attitude toward her father and the memory of her mother's strong faith in God. While listening to my grandmother, I was thinking how a loving, merciful God had protected my great-grandmother, and my grandmother that night on a mountainside with bears, mountain lions, snakes and all kinds of harm around them. Undoubtedly, God had a plan for all of our lives as well as my children and grandchildren. This particular story was shared in September 2002 while visiting my grandmother, Cora Turner Riley Snoddy, on her 92nd birthday.

My daddy was a good daddy. I loved my daddy. He was a wonderful man. But when he got that moonshine whiskey in him, he was different. One memory continues to return even though it happened when I was just a little girl. Mom and I were sitting in the house where I was raised in Buckhorn, Kentucky. We heard him coming up the road on his horse. We knew he was drunk because he was yelling. Mom said, "Come on, hurry we must get up the mountain to the orchard before he sees us. He can't make it up the hillside in his condition. We'll be OK. The Lord will help us. Hurry!"

It was pitch black outside and cold at night in the mountains. It was in the fall of the year, and the sun had already gone down behind the mountain in front of our house. We quickly started up the hillside to the orchard, the leaves rustling all around us. Mom was praying to God as we climbed and asked Him to send His angels to protect us from the rattlesnakes. The orchard was well known for its rattlesnake den. She told me the angels would make sure the snakes were all gone before we got to the top of the mountain. Suddenly the rustling sound of the leaves stopped, and it was quiet. Mom was thanking God for protecting us. She then embraced me with her warmth since we had not taken the time to dress properly for the cold temperature. Time after time, she assured me we would be alright. We slept there all night until the sun started coming up over the top of the mountain. Mom woke me, and we safely made our way home to find that our daddy had found his way home and into bed. We were safe once more from the effects of the moonshine whiskey.

I knew she had just shared a very special gift with me, a gift of faith, a faith that overpowers the gripping fear that tries to overtake us in times of trouble. When trouble rises, I will remember this story and the faith of my great-grandmother. I want to remember what God says in Psalms 34:7-"The angel of the Lord, encampeth round about them that fear him, and delivereth them."

They've Come For Me

My great-great grandmother, Nancy Bowling Turner, rested in her bed at her home in Buckhorn, Kentucky. It was April I940. Her two daughters from her first husband, my great-grandmother Sally and great-aunt Jalie, were caring for her. She was 98 years old. Her first husband, my great-great grandfather John Turner, was killed in the Civil war. After his death she had married John Stamper, and they had several more children.

Nancy had lain in her bed for several days now, and the family had gathered around. It seemed as if death was very near. She told them of hearing beautiful music playing in the background. "Can't you hear it?" she would ask. It was music that only she could hear. "Can't you see the angels?" Only she could see the angels all around the room-in the windows and hovering around her bed.

As death came closer she started talking to her children again. She described three big angels at the window with John. "They've come for me," she said while apparently looking and seeing beyond what was in the room. Her son Elijah was so distraught. He asked, "Mom which John is it?" She said, "It is John Turner." Then she passed from this life. Her son was crying out for he had hoped she had seen John Stamper, his father. He knelt by her bed and sobbed wanting to ask her more questions, but she no longer was able to hear or answer him. He was inconsolable due to thinking his father had not been with the angels who came for his mother.

Cora, my 92-year-old grandmother, related this story to me. She then went on to explain her grandmother Nancy was a devout Christian. She always handmade and wore long, black silk dresses as well as a shawl and bonnet to church. Nancy took it upon herself to provide a supply of new towels for the foot washing services at their Baptist Church in Buckhorn, Kentucky. My Grandmother Cora recalled washing her grandmother Nancy's feet and drying them on a soft new towel when she was a young girl. As she finished, her grandmother Nancy began to shout and praise the Lord as the congregation began singing "The Old Rugged Cross." It was obviously a beautiful and wonderful experience with the memory of it still very clear in her mind.

My mother told me from the time I was very small that an angel watches over me. I have always believed this! The word of God says in Psalms 91:11, "For He shall give His angels charge over thee, to keep thee in all thy ways." I thank God for a mother that instilled an unwavering faith in God and for three generations of grandmothers who passed on their heritage of faith.

I am so thankful to still have my grandmother Cora who prays constantly for her family and gives praise to God for all He has done. I have been so blessed to be able to share these special times with her as she shares her life's stories with me.

Special Note: My prayer today, Mother's Day 2003, is that when the angels come for me I will have left this legacy of faith and trust in God to my children and grandchildren. A mother can give no greater gift than to equip her children to lead a victorious and eternal life in Christ.

My Great-Great-Grandmother
Nancy Bowling Turner holding large Bible

Great-Grandmother's Porch

I remember the long wooden porch that extended across the back of great-grandmother Sally's house in Kentucky. It was a special and unique place for many reasons. On one end was a barrel with a nesting hen in it. Our oldest son Darrell got the surprise of his young life one day. While peeking into the barrel a huge chicken flew out at him. He cried hysterically. Great-grandmother Sally held him on her lap and explained that the chicken was going to have baby chicks-that the chicken was more scared of him than he was of it. She soon had him smiling again although he didn't sneak another peek that summer.

Located on the porch were an abundance of chairs, most of them handmade with hand-woven seats, roughly made benches and two or three rockers. There were small tables with blooming flowers and plants growing. The churn was usually sitting there in the sun on butter churning days. A clothesline was strung across one end from post to post where she hung her clothes to dry after washing them in the wringer washer.

On the opposite end of the porch was the boxed-in well. In order to draw water from the well, you put a bucket onto the hook. With a rope you let the bucket down, filled it, drew it back up by turning a crank and then unhooked the bucket of cool water. Many times my brothers and I would forget to hook it to one side, and the bucket would fall down into the well and have to be fished out. We always got a scolding for our carelessness. I took a picture early one morning of my great-grandmother drawing water from the well as the sun was coming up over the mountain in front of the house. Her long braided hair was not yet wound into the usual bun she wore at the nape of her neck. She was drawing the water to start breakfast which was a feast that required a lot of preparation time.

The porch was up on stilts. The myth behind these stilts was that it kept the snakes from getting into the house. Our mother told us how the chickens liked to go under there and lay their eggs. When she was a little girl they would send her under there to gather the eggs. She always moved fast because of her fear of snakes. The steps up to the porch were huge rocks that had been positioned into place. As a child I was barely able to climb up the steps. Most of the time I crawled up them. It was faster. I didn't venture too far off the porch for fear of encountering a deadly rattler.

The porch was where we gathered each morning after clearing the breakfast table. We sat, chatted, and broke beans or peeled potatoes, cleaned chickens for dinner or whatever else we needed to do. Much of the day was centered around food preparation. Usually I got the chore of churning the butter and learned to do it really well. I would churn the butter by moving the wooden dasher up and down at a steady speed until the butter started forming on top. My mother or grandmother would remove the top. Then they would take a spoon and dip the butter into a bowl, add salt and take a wooden butter paddle and form the butter by beating and pressing the excess milk out of it while forming a round firm butter mold. It was placed in the springhouse before refrigeration. At our house we used a gallon size churn that had a hand crank. It was much easier and faster than the dasher method.

When visiting in the summer, company was coming and going continuously. We saw all the relatives and cousins we hardly knew from one year to the next. Everyone was growing up and older so quickly. We would all gather on the porch. I loved to sit and listen to the stories and laughter and tales of times long ago. One summer I remember having pink eye. Mother was putting medicine in my eyes, and my whole visit was spent looking through tiny slits in my swollen eyes with my cousins teasing because I couldn't participate in any of their fun. I really didn't care all that much because I listened to the grown-ups as they played their guitars, banjoes, and fiddles while they sang their sad, lonesome songs about far away places and things I didn't understand. It stirred my heart. Daddy had a high, clear voice. He could out sing and out play all the others. They always begged him to sing one more song before everyone started their journey home. I would usually fall asleep on one of the benches or the floor of the porch and wake up the next day with mosquito bites that were treated with pink calamine lotion.

There was no indoor plumbing, and I was terrified to go to the outhouse by myself. The fear of copperheads and rattlesnakes was drilled into us so strongly that it took a powerful urge of nature to get me down that path. My grandmother felt so sorry for me. She allowed me to use her private little porcelain pot in the house, and she would even empty it. I was always so grateful. We never informed my brothers who had to make the dreaded trip down the path or go behind the trees. I would not go behind the trees even in an emergency. I was much too modest. Besides, that's where the snakes lived!

Bathing was another problem. We had to heat the water on the stove and wash from a big white porcelain basin in grandmother's spare bedroom. This I didn't mind too much, but everyone was always yelling for me to hurry up. My brothers still talk about how I hogged the bathroom at home when we finally had indoor plumbing. I filled the tub with bubble bath, locked the doors and took my time. They learned to discreetly go behind the trees in our yard until I came out. My dad had difficulty understanding why his teenage daughter needed to wash her hair every night while spending hours in the bathroom doing whatever girls do to make themselves beautiful.

How I would love to go back to Buckhorn, Kentucky and sit on that porch again. In my mind I still can. I can still smell that cool mountain air and feel the chill of the cool night breeze against my skin; I can still smell the wood smoke from the chimney after supper was cooked; I can still taste the sulfur water that always made me sick after a couple of days; I can still smell the lye soap that the towels had been washed in. I remember how my grandfather smelled of sweat, chewing tobacco, moonshine or beer and how my grandmother smelled of soap, flour, fried apples and cinnamon, fried chicken- all the things that made going to her house so special. Most of all, I can feel the love. That is what drew me then and draws me now-a place that I can go to, a place of precious memories, great-grandmother's porch.

My father Clifton W. Blake, age 16, with his first guitar

Great-Grandmother's Table

My great-grandmother's table was a long harvest table which was handcrafted by family members with handmade benches on each side and a pair of chairs on each end. It could easily seat 12 people and sometimes 14 or more if necessary. It was located in the center of the small dining room off the kitchen. The only decoration was a long, narrow still life picture of fruit that hung on the wall behind one end of the table. It was the place where we all gathered for the most delicious food ever eaten. As I was growing up, our family went to visit at least once a year during our July vacation time and around my grandmother's birthday. Don and I continued this tradition for eleven years after we married. Our sons, Darrell and Jon, were blessed to have experienced many of the same things I had as a child.

Great-grandmother Sally would rise very early in the morning and go out and kill chickens to fry for breakfast. If she didn't fix them for breakfast, we would have fried chicken for lunch. She would also shake the apple tree and gather the apples in her apron. Sometimes we children would be up early and help gather them. She would cut the apples in quarters and place them in a big cast-iron skillet filled with homemade butter, add brown sugar and cinnamon and cook them until they melted in our mouths. While the apples were cooking she would make her homemade biscuits in her hand hewn wooden dough bowl. She always kept flour in it and would make a well in the center of the bowl; add the lard, salt, baking powder and buttermilk. Then she would take her hand and mix until it felt like the right consistency. She would pinch them off, pat them into the darkened pan and place them in the woodstove oven to bake (yes, a wood stove heated up for cooking in July). While these were baking, she would fry up the bacon, sausage, or Kentucky ham and make gravy with the bits of meat and grease left in the skillet. The freshly gathered eggs were her specialty. She turned them with a spoon when cooking, and they were always perfect. When everyone was seated, she would put a large platter of eggs on the table with the soft eggs on one side and the hard eggs on the other. I don't remember her fixing them any other way. They were delicious. I've tried my whole married life to fix eggs tasting as good as hers but have never succeeded. The biscuits came out of the oven, golden brown and perfectly shaped. Her breakfast was probably my favorite meal, at least until lunchtime.

The noon meal was the largest meal of the day. After the breakfast table was cleared, the morning was spent preparing for the noon meal. The chickens were dressed and cut up for frying. The beans were picked and broken for cooking. The corn was picked and cleaned for cutting off of the cob and then fried in butter. She would also cook a hen for chicken and dumplings. I can still see those huge platters of golden fried chicken and the huge bowl of chicken and dumplings. The dumplings were made in the wooden dough bowl also by her skilled hand. She would cut them in strips and place them in the boiling broth one at a time. We had cornbread made from the corn that had been raised on the farm and taken to the mill to be ground or that had been ground by hand. She always turned it out on a plate and cut it in squares. Added to this delicious meal was wilted lettuce, green onions, cucumbers, pickled beets, freshly churned butter, her homemade jellies and jams. Then, the meal was finished off with delicious homemade pies and cobblers. Our family always took a huge birthday cake from the bakery, and she thought of the cake as a very special treat. We also took watermelons. She especially liked cold watermelon and looked forward to them each summer. They were placed in the springhouse to cool.

The dining room table would be filled with food and drink, and the men would be called to come to the table. The women would wait on the men keeping glasses filled with lemonade and cups filled with strong hot coffee. After the men had eaten, the children were called to the table and were fed. The women then settled down at the table. They spent a good deal of time talking and laughing while sharing stories of their children and gardens and how many quarts of vegetables they had canned so far that summer. They took their time eating, cleaning up and washing the dishes. It was their time together before joining the men and children out on the porch.

The rest of the afternoon would be spent on the porch visiting with relatives. We would serve them freshly made lemonade and catch up on all the family gossip. My great aunt Jalie was one of my favorites. She laughed all the time and never stopped talking. She sat and rocked while talking and laughing the afternoon away. When I was a small girl, I would sit with the women and listen to their stories instead of playing with the other children. My mother told of the time, when I was around five years of age, that I came home and promptly gave my other grandparents the complete account of my cousin's birthing experience including the push, push, pushing. My paternal grandparents, who did not talk of these things in public, were not appreciative of my newly learned knowledge and thought it was outrageous. My mother could not believe how I remembered word for word everything stated that day and how I would repeat it to anyone willing to listen. Afterwards, I was sent outside to play whenever the grown-ups talked about certain subjects.

The days seemed to end so quickly. Sometimes we visited our cousins who lived just up the road. They had horses and mules. We took turns riding in their handmade wagon pulled by a team of mules. As evening came there in the mountains of Kentucky, the sun would fall behind the mountain in front of their house and darkness would quickly fall. The cool breeze felt good after a hot, sultry July day. We would all gather around the table again for leftover chicken, biscuits, cornbread and milk. Daddy's favorite supper was cornbread crumbled in a glass of buttermilk. After eating the day's leftovers, we headed out to the porch again. Usually the aunts, uncles and cousins would come and bring their musical instruments. They would sit and play and sing for hours until everyone was voiceless and physically spent always promising to drop by tomorrow or to write and keep in touch. The children would play games or sit and listen to the music until they fell asleep.

My great-grandmother's table was not only a place that nourished our bodies but also a place that nourished our souls. It would be a place we would come back to year after year and yearn for in our hearts long after we had to say our final goodbyes.

Great-Grandmother's Quilts

While recently visiting with my grandmother Cora, my husband and I were blessed to hear several more stories about her childhood and her mother, my great-grandmother Sally Woods. I had assumed that my great-grandmother was unable to read or write. In later years when I knew her, she had others read for her and write her letters. However, this was not due to illiteracy but an eye condition. She had ingrown eyelashes that had to be hand plucked on a regular basis and caused a great deal of pain. I can remember my mother doing this when we would visit as well as several of my aunts and cousins. When I was a small girl, I would sit on the big porch next to them and wince every time they pulled one out. It made a lasting impression, and I prayed I would never have to endure such a procedure.

Grandma Cora shared that my great-grandmother could read and write and had acted as the school principal for twenty years for the small school where my grandmother and then later my mother attended. She hired and fired the schoolteachers and gave them room and board if they did not have a place to stay. For extra pay she would do their laundry. The state paid her additional money for keeping records. She also was responsible for buying supplies for the school including a truckload of handmade child size chairs for the children in the lower grades. I am fortunate to have one of those chairs that my Dad got when they tore the school down. He got four of them since I had three brothers at the time. We all still have them today. They are just as sturdy as they were all those years ago. My grandmother explained to me in great detail how they were made. She feels she could make them herself if provided the wood. It was just a matter of soaking the wood and then weaving the seats. It is amazing how she remembers all the little details.

Great-grandmother Sally also had another job. She went to the homes in the area and prepared their deceased loved ones for burial. She bathed them, clothed them and even sewed linings for their caskets if requested. Many of them were buried in pine boxes in those days. She also made shrouds for the infants who passed away, many of which perished due to burns from open fireplaces. Grandma Cora said she never turned anyone down, regardless of the circumstances. It was a gift and a service. As she was talking, I understood more clearly the history of the quilt that she had given us as a wedding gift. It was sewn with heavy velvet and materials that came from casket linings. I loved the quilt and used it all the years my boys were growing up. It went everywhere with us-car trips, ball games, the park, and on the bed of the one who was sick with a fever or flu. I still have it although it is now retired. It is safely stowed away in a pillowcase in our closet to preserve it forever. It was becoming frayed, and I became concerned about washing it one more time. It has brought our family much comfort through the years. I wish sometimes I had stored it and not used it, but I know that was not my great-grandmother's intention. It has brought comfort and many warm fuzzy memories to our family.

Grandma Cora also gave me a quilt as a wedding gift that my great-grandmother Sally had hand stitched very early in life. The batting in the quilt was cotton raised on the farm in Kentucky. I have never used this quilt, and it remains in very good condition. It is a prized possession to be passed on to my granddaughter Jessica. I do not sew or quilt; I was not blessed with that gift although they all tried to teach me. I will just have to pass down other gifts.

I've been blessed to know and to have the close and loving relationships with my grandparents throughout my life, especially my grandmothers. They have shaped and molded my life in so many ways. Their hands have helped piece together my life's quilt-one that will keep me warm in the winters of my life and one that will wrap tightly around me as I prepare to take my journey home.

Short Story Six

Grandmother's Apron

Grandmother put her apron on each morning on top of her freshly ironed cotton dress. She always kept a nice clean one waiting on a hook near the stove and only removed it when company came or at the end of the day.

Grandmother's apron served many purposes. She used it to gather apples from the tree in the yard which would be used for delicious apple pies or for drying on a screen. The dried apples would be used at a later time for stacked dried apple pies. She would use her apron to gather eggs or even to gather up the baby chicks that had strayed and would place chicken feed in her uplifted apron for us to grab and throw out to the chickens. We would stand and watch them peck and cluck their thank you until it was time to head back to the house or off for another adventure. Sometimes she would place potatoes in the big pockets or green beans and onions from the garden. On her way back to the house, she might add a few flowers to place on the kitchen table or on the window ledge.

As children, we sometimes got a dreaded spit bath with the corner of the apron and an admonition from Grandma to stay out of trouble and away from dirt. She would even shine our shoes with it before Sunday school. It was a place to hide from big brothers who were chasing and promising to kill whoever had messed with their stuff. It gave comfort to the embarrassed child who had just lost their front teeth and was being teased. Her apron would be wrapped around the small child that was hurt or cold. Noses were wiped, as well as tears, from the eyes of the grandchild who didn't want to go to bed or who didn't want to go home. She also used it to chase away the bees and flies from the sleeping babies.

When we were sitting out on the porch, grandma used her apron to fan herself from the heat. There was always a handkerchief handy in her apron pocket to dry her tears when she was sad or really happy. I can still see her standing in the yard with her apron to her face as our car backed out and headed down the road for home. The time with her slipped by so quickly. It would be a whole year before visiting her again. Wonderful memories filled our lives.

Special Note: My husband's mother always wore an apron. She had quite a collection of them from plain to fancy. Our granddaughter Jessica was named after her Grandmother Jessie. After she passed away, I kept some of her aprons to be given to Jessica as a keepsake. I asked her one day while she was visiting if she would like one of Grandma Jessie's aprons. "YEAH!" she replied with much enthusiasm. She then looked up at me and asked, "Nana, what is an apron anyway?" This story is for my granddaughter Jessica who hopefully has a better understanding now of an apron. I suspect there are many of us who would gladly trade our cell phones and computers for the corner of a Grandmother's apron.

L. to R. Jon, Great-Grandmother
Sally, Darrell, July 1970

Get On Up The Road

My great-grandmother, Sally Turner Woods, was a quiet woman who seldom smiled, was a hard worker and methodically went about her daily chores. She was married the second time to John Woods after the death of her first husband. John was a drinker, not much of a worker. He would walk miles to buy moonshine and to be with his drinking buddies.

One evening a couple of his buddies came calling. They had consumed all of the moonshine on hand and had no money between them to buy more. John wanted more moonshine and informed his buddies about where they could get the money. He told them my great-grandmother kept her money in a pouch she wore around her waist, but he would need their help in getting it. They all agreed on a plan to accost my great-grandmother and rob her.

Little did they know, she had been listening to this conversation from behind the door. Quietly she went into her bedroom and got her pistol which had never been fired. She loaded it, placed it under her apron, sat down in her rocker and waited for them.

They all walked in together with John demanding her money. She refused! He restated his intention to take it one-way or the other. He wanted it immediately! She stood up. When he reached for her, she pulled out the pistol, aimed it and started shooting at their feet. They started dancing, dodging the bullets that were flying all around them. The two drinking buddies headed up the road as fast as they could run. John was soon sober and a little more respectful of Sally Woods. Fearing a repeat performance from my great-grandmother, he never mentioned her money again.

She didn't have to worry about the drinking buddies coming around again because they knew she meant business. She gained quite a reputation around those parts of Kentucky after that incident. Somehow I can see her long faded work dress, apron and old fashioned black heeled shoes, her long braided hair balled up at the nape of her neck, standing firm and unsmiling stating with pistol in hand, "Get on up the road!"

Sally's daughter Cora, my grandmother, related this account to me on October 16, 2003. When my great-grandmother's death was imminent, she shared more information about the money belt. It was for her funeral and burial expenses. My grandmother presented it to the bank without opening it. All the bank employees gathered to examine a very unusual and unique pile of money. It was a first and probably a last experience for all of them. It was a large quantity of molded bills. No one knows how many years she had saved and worn the money on her person.

Great-grandmother Sally passed away in February 1972 at the age of 84. I was in nursing school at the time, but we made the trip back to Buckhorn for her funeral at the Bob Gabbard Funeral Home in Jackson. I don't remember much of the sermon, but I'll never forget the two ladies who sang acapella in that mournful mountain sound. I had chills all over my body. My mother and I just held each other and wept with grief. When I said my goodbyes at her casket, I bent over and kissed her on the cheek and patted her beautiful white hair. I wanted to touch her one last time. She was buried in the Stamper Cemetery in Morris Fork which was straight up a mountain. It was a snowy and icy morning. My husband, one of the pallbearers, thought he would have a heart attack before they made it to the top. He was in his early 30's at the time but carrying her casket straight up that mountain was one of the hardest things he has ever performed physically.

After our marriage and before her death, we spent eleven summers with her. All the relatives would gather every year to celebrate her July 12th birthday. We had no idea how much we would miss her and that time together as a family. It was an end to an era, a time that would never be again-only in precious memories.

Portrait I painted of my Great-Grandmother Sally
Turner Woods in 1984

SECTION II

What happened to that young girl who ran and jumped and climbed trees? She was so light, lithe and tan. She ran barefoot down the lane only to run back again and again singing as she ran, "Yes Jesus Loves Me."

Rooster

There were few real dangers or fears growing up on the farm, but one comes to mind that still makes me shudder. Rooster was huge and white with a large, bright red comb that would flop around when he ran.

It seemed he was everywhere! No matter where we tried to go he would wait until we were almost there, and here he would come chasing us trying to flog us with his spurs. It was a terrifying experience for four small children. We all hated Rooster. I'm sure Rooster chasing us, and our fear of him catching and killing us, interrupted our peaceful dreams at night.

We did not have indoor plumbing. It was particularly difficult for us to reach the outhouse because we had to get past Rooster who seemingly had eyes in the back of his head. He would wait until we were too far from the house but not quite close enough to the outhouse for safety. Here he would come running as fast as his little chicken legs could go. Many trips to the outhouse were postponed until a later and safer time.

My two youngest brothers, Darrell and Ronnie, were his favorite targets because they couldn't run as fast. One day he attacked our brother Darrell and had him on the ground. Thankfully he was not seriously injured, but my mother was furious with Rooster. He may have been our only rooster, but his time was short. When our Dad came home from work that night, Rooster was caught and taken to the chopping block where he was beheaded.

Mother prepared him the next day for dinner. We had a large kettle of Rooster and dumplings. The meat was tough. But what could you expect, he had become quite muscular chasing us all day long. The dumplings as I remember were delicious. What a relief-Rooster was finally gone!

The Outhouse

The outhouse, or "necessary" as some called it, was part of our childhood growing up on a farm in the 1950's. We had a two seater! It sat on a hill that sloped down on the back side into what we called a "holler."

I never liked the outhouse. It seemed I always had company during my visits. The bees, birds, spiders, bugs of all kinds and of course the possibility of a dreaded snake were my companions. If you ran out of paper, you could yell for an hour for someone to "pleeeaasssee" bring a roll of paper. Usually our busy mother had to take time out to do this because my siblings ignored the pleas.

Visiting the outhouse at night was always a problem. I was afraid to go out into the dark night by myself which meant I had to use whatever method worked at the moment (usually tears and begging) to get my older brother Roger to go too. It was unthinkable to be in the outhouse in total darkness; so, he would stand in front of the door holding the flashlight back through a crack in the door. This was always frustrating for both of us as I was always accusing him of looking, and he of course adamantly denied it.

My brother Roger tells this story much better than I do-embellishing it to make everyone feel sorry for him due to being dragged from his warm bed in the middle of the night to escort his sister to the outhouse. He was my hero, my protector. I always felt safe with him leading the way down the path to the outhouse with the big flashlight. Of course, whatever was lurking out there in the darkness would get him first giving me time to run for the safety of our house. Regardless, I will never forget the "outhouse experience!"

The Sack Man

My first memory of my Grandmother Cora's home is my mother lying in bed holding my new baby brother Roger in her arms with my dad at her side in the back bedroom of my grandparents' farmhouse. I was standing in the doorway peeking in at them. I was 18 months old. I still have that picture in my mind as if I had just taken the snapshot. I don't know if it is unusual to have memory at such an early age, but the reason this one stuck in my memory bank so clearly is that from that day forward my world was never the same. I think maybe I was jealous about being pushed out of the nest a little too early. My Dad loves to tell how I would climb out of bed, steal Roger's bottle and take it back to bed. My bottom was warmed many times for that little deed. As my brother grew we became inseparable, like twins really. My thought processes were a little ahead of his (still are-gotcha Roger), and I got him into a lot of trouble with our Dad. Years later he paid me back by getting me into trouble with Mother. Our noses were in one of the corners of the living room almost every day.

I can remember at the age of four playing in the corncrib at my grandparents' farmhouse with tiny green dishes that belonged to my Aunt Mildred. I loved those dishes. One day I decided to put some real food into them from our dog Hootie's dish. The only problem with this plan was Hootie was eating lunch at the time and proceeded to defend his territory by taking a chunk out of my right leg at the knee. The hollering and the blood was enough to bring everyone running. Daddy had our only automobile at work. My Uncle Henry carried me across the cornfield, with my mother close behind, to the neighbor's house. I was taken to the doctor and stitched up. From that moment to this day I've had a fear of big dogs. My Grandfather John threatened to shoot the dog, but my Dad talked him out of it since it was my fault and not the dog's. We even ended up taking Hootie with us to our farm as a watchdog. He was a good one. He would have defended us from the devil himself. He fought a black snake one day and was bitten on the tongue. I can still see that snake all coiled up and striking out at him, but he would not give up.

My grandparents moved to Metamora, Indiana and lived in a house on highway 52 when I was about six years old. It was a very nice house, and we loved to go visit. A drive-in restaurant was just a few feet from the house, and our grandparents would buy us orange dreamsicles. We looked so forward to getting those and a coke in a bottle with a straw. There were four of us now. I had three brothers to look after and keep up with-Roger, Darrell, and Ronald. We would sometimes spend the night at Grandma Cora's. She would have us lie on the bed sideways, all four of us. I can remember how hard it was to go to sleep because of the traffic on the highway. We lived on a remote farm with no traffic; and, the only noise we heard at night was the whippoorwills, katydids, tree frogs and sometimes a hoot owl or a hound dog that had treed a coon. We would lie there and giggle and talk and wonder what our parents were doing. Grandma could only take so much of that before telling us to shut up and go to sleep, or the sack man would come and get us. We never knew for sure who the sack man was, but she made him sound really scary. Sometimes if we still didn't settle down, she would tell us she heard Peewee coming. He was a local hobo, and so we quickly settled down. Her tactics always worked. We knew causing too much trouble would diminish our chances of receiving dreamsicles and cokes the next day.

Our Grandpa John passed away shortly after he and our Grandma Cora moved to nearby Laurel, Indiana by the railroad track. I was getting older, around 12 now. When we would visit and get on her last nerve, she would tell us she could hear the sack man coming down the railroad track. Even at the age of 12 or 13 and knowing there was no such thing as the sack man, it still gave me the "creeps."

Several years later I married and had two small boys. One day they were being unusually rowdy. In desperation I looked at them and said, "If you boys don't shut up and settle down the sack man is going to come and get you and carry you away." They just looked at me and then at each other, laughed and continued on with what they were doing-so much for old-fashioned scare tactics. It just is not effective with this new generation. It sure worked for Grandma Cora. When I think about it, was it the sack man or Grandma Cora who convinced us? She had a way with words; yet, she always had nickels and dimes for cokes and dreamsicles!

On Grandma Cora's 93rd birthday, her grandson Bob Swininger and wife Vicky hosted a huge family gathering in her honor. It was a wonderful celebration of life. She was frail but able to walk and many pictures were taken. She looked so pretty. We are so blessed to still have her. I can't remember so many people and so much food in the many years that we have been getting together. It was a good, good day with lots of laughter and reminiscing. I asked a couple of my cousins that day if they remembered the sack man. They smiled, nodded and said, "Oh yeah."

Special Note: I recently learned from talking with my Grandma that the sack man character originated from an elderly man who frequently walked the railroad tracks with a large sack on his back. Some say he still does!

Rena and L. to R. Roger, Darrell, Ronald

I Want My Mommy

This is probably one of the most painful memories of my childhood. I was only four years old, but the memory of that long ago day is a painful and traumatic one. I remember the big, black, shiny car with two men and my mother getting out of it. My mother opened her arms, and I ran into them. I wrapped my arms around her neck and my legs around her waist and hung tightly onto her. My two-year-old brother Roger was holding onto her skirt. She was crying. The two men were trying to console her. We were in the yard at my paternal grandparents' home, and they were standing by as was my Aunt Craten. I'm not sure how long we had been there. Daddy apparently was at work. I don't remember him being there that day.

After several minutes had passed with my mother trying to stop our crying, the two men walked over and told her it was time. She tried to set me down but couldn't get me to let go. My grandmother and my Aunt Craten unwound my body from hers and took my brother's hand and led us away to the house. My mother was sobbing loudly as the two men led her back to the big, black car. Then she was gone!

I was screaming, "I want my mommy, I want my mommy, I don't want to stay here." I remember my aunt holding and rocking me back and forth in the big rocking chair by the wood stove. She kept repeating over and over that it was going to be alright. I probably cried myself to sleep. For some reason, I have no further memory of that day and very little of the next three months.

It was important to understand what had happened leaving me so traumatized. I felt that my mother had somehow abandoned and left me there with people I really didn't know that well. Despite pushing it from my mind for years, it would always creep back. I think for many years I feared losing my mother again. Mother and I had a good relationship as I was growing up. She always took the time to listen to her children's questions and problems and tried to explain things. I shared everything with her, well, almost everything. I wanted to know what had happened that day, and I finally got up the courage to request specific details when I was a teenager. She explained it as honestly as she could and with many tears.

She and my dad had separated with a nasty divorce after a court hearing. Daddy had acquired custody, and Mother was given visitation rights. The memory had been of her first visit with us accompanied by the pastors of the church where she attended. It had been as traumatic for her as it was for us. My dad took us to see her as much as he could. In just a short time they were remarried.

To my knowledge it was just not discussed through the years. It was as if it had not happened. I was the only daughter and the oldest with six brothers following.

I never let her or my dad know how much I hurt. Once old enough to understand I realized it was not her fault. She had been hurting as much or more. Divorce is a painful thing for adults, but it is often much more painful for the children who somehow are caught in a tangle of feelings and emotions that may take them years or their whole lives to work through.

I am blessed because my parents loved each other and made a life that was a happy, if not ideal one, for their children. After their reconciliation we faithfully attended church together. One of my fondest memories is waking in the morning to see Mother sitting on the sofa, after getting Daddy off to work, reading her Bible. Each morning, as she sent the four oldest off to school, she lined us up at the door, kissed us good-bye and told us she was praying for us. The prayers of my mother, no doubt, are still being felt and answered today. Thank you God for good parents and good happy memories that have overshadowed any bad ones. My parents were married 52 years before my mother passed February 27, 1996.

When things get really difficult and I'm feeling the stresses of life pulling, I find myself tearing up and thinking, "I want my Mommy." Regardless of our age, we still in many ways want to be held in the arms of our mothers. I miss her so much. I look forward to the day when we will be together again for all eternity, and we will never have to part.

Rena age 4 and brother Roger age 2 at the home of
their grandparent's James T. and Mary Ann Blake

Daddy's Little Helpers

Our daddy was a very busy man. He was a farmer and also a factory worker. Planting and harvesting the garden took up a great deal of his time. As we grew older the chores on the farm became a family affair.

Daddy did most of the gardening. He ploughed the quarter-acre garden plot behind our house with a team of horses for the first few years after we moved to the farm. After the ground was ploughed and disced he would lay off the rows. We were allowed to help drop the seed and then cover them. Watering was our biggest and most important chore. We would take turns pumping and then carrying buckets of water to the garden where we would dip out the water and carefully water each plant and row.

One day our helping got us into a lot of trouble. Daddy had run out of time that day; so, he placed the tomato plants in a bucket of water under a shade tree to be planted later. Roger and I decided we'd help him out (my idea) by planting his tomato plants and surprising him. We picked out what we thought was the perfect spot across the road on the hillside. With our hands, we dug little holes just like we had seen our Daddy do many times. In each hole we placed the tomatoes, and soon they were all in the ground. We headed back to the house bursting with pride and anticipation of how proud Daddy would be of his little helpers. We might even get a nickel or dime for doing such a good job.

When Daddy came home that evening and reached the top of the hillside, something caught his eye. It looked a lot like his tomato plants lying on the ground wilting in the heat of the hot sun from their lack of water (OOPS, we forgot the watering part). To say he was upset is a great understatement. Mother was shocked to hear of our gardening escapade. Our anticipation of our Daddy's surprise and happiness quickly faded while being replaced by a question of where we could hide and fast.

As I recall, my brother Roger got the scolding of his young life and a good spanking. He tried to tell Daddy that it was my idea, but Daddy just wouldn't believe I could do such a thing. I didn't try very hard to convince him otherwise. Roger held that one against me for a long, long time!

Paper Dolls

Like most little girls, I loved playing with paper dolls. I had a large collection of them in a shoebox. Many of them were gifts from my parents and grandparents. I also cut out the ones featured in a weekly Cincinnati newspaper. I spent hours dressing and undressing them. This was one playtime I didn't have to share with anyone. My brothers didn't want any part of my paper dolls!

I was in the first grade now, and I decided one day to take my paper doll collection to our two-room country school. We could play with them at recess and lunch. I was so excited about showing them to my friends.

After arriving at school I placed the box in my desk for safekeeping. I stuck my hand inside my desk and kept it on the box inside. With the other hand, I picked up my pencil and started writing the letters of the alphabet.

Our teacher was a large woman with gray curly hair and appeared to be quite elderly. She spoke harshly and demanded our respect with the threat of the large paddle stationed across the front of her desk. It was always before our eyes as a reminder to be on our best behavior, or we would pay the consequences.

I was happily working away when I suddenly became aware of the teacher's presence at my side. I froze as I heard these words, "What do you have in your desk?" She was standing over me with her hands on her hips. I couldn't make my voice come out of my throat. I just looked up at her and didn't move my hand from inside my desk. She reached into my desk, grabbed my box, and after looking inside, hurled it into the wood stove in the middle of the room. I was shocked! I couldn't believe my eyes. I tried very hard not to cry, but my heart was broken. My beloved paper dolls were burned and gone forever.

Even now after 54 years have gone by I can still feel the sting of her cruelty. I went home that afternoon and tearfully explained to my mother what had happened. Mother reminded me that I should not have taken them to school, and it was a lesson to remember and not forget. She was right. I never have!

Lost in the Cornfield

Being raised on a farm in a remote rural area in the 1950's was always an adventure and at times very difficult. Daddy worked two jobs all the years we lived on the farm. He worked the 3-pm-11-pm shift in a factory, traveled an hour each way and farmed during the day. His day began at 4:00 am with milking the cows. We all had our chores, and mother milked the cows in the evening.

Our five-year-old brother Darrell was a farmer at heart. He tagged along with Daddy every chance he got. He especially liked riding on the tractor with Daddy to the cornfield. One afternoon he asked to go with Daddy to the cornfield on the tractor. Daddy, being busy and wanting to get his chores done, refused his request. My brother was very upset. When Daddy was out of sight, he took off on his own walking out away from the house and toward the cornfield. No one thought much about it since we often played in the woods next to the cornfield.

Daddy came in for supper, but Darrell was nowhere to be found. Everyone was becoming alarmed now because it would soon be dark. There were no streetlights, only a security light on the barn. When darkness fell it was very black. At this point we were all in a panic. We walked up and down and back and forth over every play area and hideaway we could think of, calling his name as loudly as we could.

Our grandparents, who lived a mile away, and our neighbors were called to help us in the search. Daddy had a hunch he had followed him to the cornfield, hoping he would give in and give him a ride on the tractor. He decided to start up and down the rows calling his name while driving alongside the cornrows blowing the car horn. After several tries, my brother finally heard the horn and stood up in the field. Daddy spotted him. Darrell had become lost in the tall corn not knowing which direction to take. He had cried and called out until he had fallen to the ground in exhaustion and finally to sleep.

Daddy was so shaken and so happy to see him that he couldn't scold him. The realization had come to him later, with Darrell lying in the field, he could easily have run over him with the car wheels. We were all so relieved to see them come out of the cornfield. Darrell had learned a valuable lesson about being disobedient. We all hugged and cried out of sheer joy and thankfulness that our brother was home safe and unharmed.

Special Note: Heavenly Father, as I write this story, I am reminded that just as my earthly father went into the cornfield searching and calling out my brother's name, I too was lost in the cornfield of sin. How thankful I am Father that I heard You call my name while realizing disobedience had separated me, Your child, from You. The Bible tells us in Luke 15:10, "There is joy in the presence of the angels of God over one sinner that repenteth."

Where Angels And "Kids" Meet

It was, as my Daddy would say a, "hotter than a firecracker" Sunday afternoon. We arrived home from church and enjoyed Mother's fried chicken with all the trimmings and a homemade chocolate cake for dessert. Daddy took off his tie and rolled up his shirtsleeves. Mother removed her Sunday shoes and put on her sandals. My brothers and I put on our play clothes and were admonished not to get dirty since we would soon be visiting our aunt and uncle and their eight children. Daddy loaded the car with two cold watermelons, four children, balls and bats and whatever else we could sneak out of the house.

As soon as we arrived at our destination, the older children began bossing the younger children around. I was eight and considered one of the older children. It was decided the older children would go down to the creek behind the house and go wading since it was so hot. Our parents warned us to not go far down stream where the water was deep and to stay within their sight. The water felt so invitingly cool. The more we waded the further out we got, away from the house and our parents. I was enjoying myself until the water got deeper, almost to my waist. Then I became frightened and informed my cousin Sue I couldn't swim. Sue reassured me and took my hand. She could swim for both of us! I started kicking my feet as she had shown me. Suddenly water was up to my chest; I panicked and lost my balance. My arms were flailing in the water while my feet and toes were stretching to feel the bottom. Unable to get hold of anything, I started to gulp mouthfuls of water as I desperately fought for air and the surface. My body became paralyzed with fear realizing death could be near. Just as I felt myself go limp, a hand grabbed my arm and pulled me up to the top. I gasped for air and started coughing. Sue hung on to me telling me to kick as hard as I could. With her help I managed to get back on my feet, wade out of the water and onto the bank. I was weak, shivering, sick from the water I had swallowed, scared and grateful to be alive all at the same time. My legs felt a little rubbery as we finally headed back to the house. Each of us swore not to tell our parents.

My aunt was a fabulous cook and always had baked treats and homemade lemonade. I watched as the little ones ate the watermelon and spit the seeds out. Watermelon juice ran down their arms and chins, and they had big grins on their faces. Mother looked my way as if questioning my refusal to eat anything. I told her I was too full to eat. It was obvious Mother could sense otherwise, but she didn't probe. I wanted to tell her about my near drowning experience-how good it felt to breathe in the warm air and just sit and feel alive. My focus switched to the little kids who were spitting watermelon seeds at each other. Everyone was laughing and having a good time. The watermelon sure looked good.

I often think of that day. Was Sue's hand the one that actually held me up, or was there someone else helping? She was younger and smaller! During that "hotter than a firecracker" Sunday afternoon, I truly believe my Guardian Angel decided to go for a nice cool swim in a country creek.

Short Story Sixteen

The Cellar

The cellar was a scary place located under one half of our house. It had been part of an original log cabin that had long since been gone from the site. It had the original rock walls and beams. Daddy had built shelves and a large bin on one wall for the potatoes.

It was my job as the eldest child and only girl to make the daily trips to the cellar where all of the canned foods and potatoes were stored. Mother had canned all of the vegetables and fruit and even meat that would feed our family through the winter until the next garden was harvested. I remember my mother canning 246 quarts of green beans one summer. I helped snap a large portion of those—my fingers will never forget.

When I was sent to the cellar my imagination always started pumping. I imagined snakes, spiders, bugs or evil beings lurking in the shadows. I moved quickly putting potatoes in the large dishpan, running up the steps to set them on the ground, then going back down for green beans, corn, tomatoes, pears, peaches or blackberries. I always ran as fast as I could to outrun the creatures waiting there for their next meal.

One Saturday morning it happened-the scene I had always played over and over in my mind. I ran up the steps and right into a huge corn snake. I screamed loudly and froze in my steps. I can still see that snake in my mind. Daddy came running out of the house. To my amazement, he picked the snake up by the tail and flung it out into the yard. He grabbed my trembling body and carried me and the green beans into the kitchen.

He sat me on a chair until I could catch my breath. Once able to talk, I repeated over and over again how I never wanted to go to the cellar again.

I was not given cellar duty for a couple of days until Mother needed a jar of this or a jar of that. Being the eldest and only girl I was once again sent to the cellar. It took all the courage I could muster. I knew for certain now that snakes liked our cellar too. Fortunately, I never had another snake encounter.

I can close my eyes even now and smell the dampness of the dirt floor and the aroma of potatoes, especially when they were first dug. We worked very hard in the garden to raise our food. The cellar kept it for us-safe and dry and with the jars all lined up neatly on the shelves. It is a beautiful place now that it is a memory and not a chore.

Grandmother Blake's House

I have always had a love for old things. I think it all started as a small child at my Grandmother Mary Ann Blake's house. My grandparents lived in a big, old Victorian era farmhouse that sat on a small hill at the end of a long tree lined lane. It was so different from the small modern type home that we lived in at the time. I loved going there because of always finding a new treasure.

I spent hours in the upstairs bedrooms looking at the massive bedroom furniture that almost reached to the ten-foot ceilings. The black walnut wardrobe that my great-grandfather built inside the house (too massive to make the stairs) was filled with vintage clothing that had been worn by my great-grandparents, grandparents and their ten children. My father was number eight in line; thus, he had older brothers and sisters starting families and working while leaving behind their childhood treasures. The wardrobe smelled of mothballs, a smell that I was not particularly fond of but tolerated. I went through drawer after drawer of beautifully hand crafted linens, baby clothes and handmade quilts.

There were five huge antique beds in the three bedrooms as well as assorted tables and dressers and chests. There were huge pictures, one of which hung over a large oak library table. It made a deep impression on me as a child. I slept in the big over-sized bed that reached almost to the ceiling. Its fluffy feather bed and quilts kept me snug, safe and warm. I would look at the picture of two people standing in a field. I knew they were praying and giving thanks but couldn't quite figure out why or what they were praying about. This picture would remind me to say my prayers too. Then I would drift off to sleep. I didn't know the name of the painting until many years later when purchasing a copy for my own home. It is called the Angelus painted by Jean-Francis Millet (1857-59.) It was placed in an antique frame and brings back happy memories of childhood days in my grandparents' home.

The parlor downstairs was filled with a beautiful hand carved oak bedroom suite. The dressers had marble tops, and the bed had a tall magnificent headboard. This is where my cousins and I would go and make up plays, acting them out and talking about boys and all the latest things. My city cousins were really snooty; yet, my country cousins and I would hang on to their every word. It seemed they had much more glamorous lives. One of my city cousins used a big word one day that I had never heard before-"facetious." I thought to myself, "I must remember that word so I can look it up." After looking up its meaning, I thought it would be a good one to try out on some of my friends at school. It became one of those words that everyone started using. "Don't be facetious" became the "in" phrase at school. Our city cousins were just a little ahead of us country folks in fashion and conversation.

My grandmother was a fanatic about cleanliness. At a very young age, I learned that if I was going to be her assistant I had to do it her way. I loved to wash and dry her beautiful George and Martha Washington dishes and place them back in the open glass cupboards that reached to the ceiling. I was warned over and over to be careful. My grandfather had brought the dishes back from a trip to Cincinnati, Ohio. I remember the day I accidentally dropped a glass and broke it. Grandmother cleaned the mess up and lectured me about being careful. Out of my nervousness, I let another one slip from my hand. I can still see the look and hear the scolding. I was sent outside to sit in the swing and was not allowed to help with the dishes for a long time.

My Grandmother tried to teach me the proper way to do things, and I was eager to learn. My biggest failure was sewing. She had me crochet granny squares over and over and rip them out. I could never get the hang of it. She tried to teach me to quilt, giving me her quilt pieces to put together; but, I could never get the ends to come out quite right. I never developed a love affair with the needle and thread.

She also tried to pass on her green thumb by giving me cuttings to take home and nurture. I seemed to always overwater them. I couldn't help myself. She would tell me to wait until they were dry to the touch, but I just had this need to water them. Over the years, I've learned that a little neglect makes for healthy flowers. I always plant pink petunias for Grandmother Blake. They were her favorite along with pink begonias. I can remember how my grandfather fussed every fall when she started bringing in the potted flowers to place in the upstairs and downstairs windows for the winter.

They had indoor plumbing several years before we did. My brothers and I were fascinated with the flushing part. We were admonished over and over again to stop flushing the toilet. I especially enjoyed the bathtub and not going to the outhouse at night. My grandfather kept his two-seater outhouse just in case there were problems with the new plumbing.

My Grandfather Blake had a specialty that he cooked every morning for breakfast. He made brown sugar syrup. It was delicious with my Grandmother's homemade biscuits. I can still see him sitting at the table eating the syrup mixed with homemade butter, spreading the mixture on hot biscuits with a knife. He drank his coffee from his saucer until it cooled down a bit. The radio was always playing in the background while they ate. On Sunday mornings they would sit in their rocking chairs by the wood stove and listen to the Cadle Tabernacle.

Supper at my grandparents' home was always the same. They ate Corn Flakes cereal. We were glad they did because of the packs of marbles that came in the cereal box. They always saved them for us, and we divided them up between the four of us. It was amazing how much fun we could have with marbles. They were early to bed and early to rise. If some of their children came to visit over the weekend they would stay up late and talk. Of course we were sent to bed, but we would creep over to the open register and sit and listen to them talk until they heard us giggling. Then we would be asked to go back to bed. We would dive into the big feather beds and soon be fast asleep.

I loved every part of grandmother's house. The big, round oak table and high backed chairs were particularly special. We would gather around this table as a family to share delicious home cooked meals and the latest gossip. It seemed that no matter how many people came by to visit, we always had room for one more at the table.

My grandparents sold their farm and had an auction six months after I was married. I was fortunate enough to buy some things at the auction. I have one of the rocking chairs that they sat in every day and my grandmother's green depression applesauce dish among other smaller items. As the beautiful antiques were being sold I wished to be rich with a huge house so I could buy it all. Many of them I do still own in my dreams. I even dream of the house sometimes, and I am always searching, looking for new treasures. With time, I have come to realize the greatest treasures in the house were my grandparents and the wonderful memories they gave me while growing up.

The Ring

I stood at my bedroom window looking out into the cold, clear winter night as I usually did each night before going to bed. This was a special time when looking up into the sky at the stars. Sometimes I would talk to God or make wishes on the brightest star.

This particular night a star caught my eye. It was huge and appeared to be very close. I was fascinated by it and had a strong urge to make a wish. I was twelve years old, and I'd never had a real ring-only the toy ones that came in the Cracker Jack box. I didn't have a particular one in mind, but I wanted it to be a nice one to wear all the time.

I stood there looking at that star, and I remembered my mother telling me it was superstitious to wish upon a star. She felt that God supplied our needs if we only asked and believed Him. I looked up at the sky again. I asked God, if He could really hear me, to please send me a ring. If He did answer my prayer, I would never wish upon a star again.

Two days after asking God for a ring, I was at my Grandmother Blake's house washing dishes. They lived a mile down the road, and I spent all the time I could there. I loved them very much and would do little chores for them. My grandmother would show me how to cook and sew and care for her dozens of flowers. Sometimes she would give me little presents or money, but mostly she would give me milk and cookies or biscuits with jelly and life lessons. She walked over to the kitchen cabinet and turned around and said, "By the way, I found this ring up in the cabinet; and, I think it might fit you. I'd like for you to have it." It was beautiful and fit perfectly. I danced around the kitchen with excitement and hugged my grandmother sharing how God really did hear my ring prayer. She laughed and shook her head as she often did.

A coincidence? Does God really hear and answer prayer? Does He really care about the desires of a twelve year old heart? Is He real?

I've never doubted for a moment since that long ago day that He is real. He loves me so much. He made Himself known to me in a special personal way. I trust Him with every fiber of my being. He's never let me down. I still stand at my windows and gaze at the stars on a clear night, seeing God and his wondrous works. He's everywhere I look.

Short Story Nineteen

A Father's Love

It was October 17, l958 on my 14th birthday-the most miserable and unhappy day of my life. My 9-year-old brother Darrell was dying, maybe even today, at this very moment. "Please God," I prayed, "help me to be strong just a little longer." I knew I'd never see him alive again. I hurt so much inside. I cried, but it didn't help. All the tears in the world would not keep him with us.

Only three short months before, I had come home late one night from a 4-H skating party to find my parents sitting in the living room on the sofa with their arms around each other. They were crying. Their faces told the story. My brother had been sick, and they had taken him to the doctor that day for tests. So when my father finally spoke, it was as if I had already heard it all before. I had dreamed a few nights before that my brother Darrell had leukemia and would die. This was God's way of preparing me, and He's done this many times since. The doctor had given them the test results immediately. Darrell had acute leukemia and was only expected to live a short time. I thought my heart would burst. We stayed there, my parents and I holding onto each other crying and praying, asking God to help us bear it and to give us strength and comfort. We prayed for a miracle-for God to spare his life if it was His will. We decided we wouldn't tell him or my smaller brothers the seriousness of the illness.

How quickly the time went by. He was given blood transfusions every two weeks at a children's hospital in Cincinnati, Ohio. Initially he would appear normal and his face would have color in it. For those few days, we would play and ride our pony and enjoy each other just like nothing was wrong. Then we would notice he would sit out the games and be short of breath and more pale with each new day. My other brothers were quick to notice and didn't push him. Even though they didn't know the name of the disease, they knew he was leaving us. I also believe he knew he was dying for there was a special closeness we all felt for one another.

Then on October 15, in the middle of the night, he hemorrhaged and started vomiting blood. He was lying on the sofa, so still and white, trying very hard to be brave. I believe he was in pain. I stood there, holding my two-year-old brother tightly to quiet his crying, wishing that I could cry, but I couldn't. I had to be brave too. I stood there looking at my brother trying to tell him with my eyes of my love for him and how sorry I was for all the times I'd fought with him—hit, kicked and screamed at him. We probably were the closest and loved each other the most, but no one would have ever thought so the way we were constantly at each other. Our parents were always saying that we were just alike, and that's why we didn't get along. That's the last thing we wanted to hear. As I stood there I knew this was the final good-bye. Oh God, how I wished it was me. I also asked God to take him quickly and not to let him suffer or to be afraid. There had been so little time to touch him and hold him and tell him that I loved him. The time had run out; it was gone. My parents were taking him to the hospital. We all gathered around him to say "good-bye, hurry and get well, and we'll see you soon." Our parents rushed us out the door and down the road to our grandparents' house a mile away. They had a long trip ahead of them, and they knew they had to get him to the hospital as quickly as possible.

Our grandparents met us at the door and gathered us in with tears in their eyes, but no one spoke a word about it. Everyone was so quiet. They quickly turned down the beds and got everyone tucked in for what was left of the night. As I snuggled up close to my little brother Greg, I couldn't help but to remember all the times I had let Darrell come into my bed and snuggle, especially these past months when he was sick and cold. I was unable to sleep that night. The next day we went to school although we didn't want to. It was decided it would be for the best. We hurried home that afternoon for news from our parents, but there was none.

I had completely forgotten that the next day was my birthday. On that afternoon my father came home, and we all rushed out to meet him for any news of our brother. He looked so tired and so serious, and then he told us that Darrell was very critical and in a coma and not expected to recover. We all cried. After a while, my father came over and put his arm around me and asked me to go for a ride with him. We ended up at the little town close by at the general store. My father said, "Happy Birthday Rena, your mother and I wanted you to be remembered on your birthday and to have something." I didn't want anything for my birthday considering the circumstances. I wanted to completely forget about it and put up a fight. But, he insisted. So he took me into the store and told me to buy whatever I wanted. I knew he probably didn't have much money because the past few months had really been hard on him financially. I looked around the store and something finally caught my eye. It was a light blue billfold with a picture of a lady with an umbrella on it. It really captured my heart. My father was pleased, and I really did like it. It didn't cost much either. I still have that billfold and cherish it because of what it represents. For many years, I didn't understand all of what had taken place that day and how it would affect my life years later. My birthdays have been reminders of that dreadful day. Then I came to the full knowledge of how much my parents must have loved me for my father to travel that great distance leaving his dying son and grieving wife to remember my birthday. How hard it must have been for my mother to let him go.

My brother died two days later on October 19, 1958. A part of us went with him, and he left a part of himself here with us. I finally shared with my parents what this had meant and how I had always known and felt their love. Out of that time of almost unbearable grief came this beautiful and cherished memory. I believe my Heavenly Father, who knows all my needs, brought it to my mind with new insight. In His infinite wisdom He knew I needed the assurance of my earthly father's love. Most importantly, I needed to be made aware again of my Heavenly Father's love.

SECTION III

Where is that young bride who walked, no floated down the aisle to meet the young man she would share herself and her life? She was so full of hopes, dreams and plans to have the most wonderful life that anyone had ever known. When so young, life seems to be forever just awaiting your next magical step.

The $50.00 Investment

Our family moved from our Franklin County farm to a large two-story house in Hartsville, Indiana. My father had taken a job with Cummins Engine Company in Columbus, Indiana. He had been driving one and one-half hours each way and farming too; so, the move was made as soon as the school year ended. It was an extremely difficult time for our family. We had recently lost our brother to leukemia, and my mother had given birth to a stillborn baby girl. I was going into my sophomore year of high school, and my three younger brothers were still in grade school.

Upon arriving in Hartsville, we were disappointed to find that there was not a local Baptist church our family could attend. Our new neighbors invited us to their church. I was eager to attend and meet the young people, whom I had been told, were very friendly and would welcome me with open arms. This, however, was not the case. I was the new girl in town, and the girls were very unfriendly that first visit. Don, my future husband, was particularly rude and unkind to me. I had just had a new permanent put in my hair that week, and it was a little too curly-maybe even a little frizzy. I sat down in my seat, and I heard him telling everyone that my hair looked like a "bird's nest." If looks could kill, the one I gave him should have done the job. He hung his head, and everyone tried not to laugh. I managed to stay in my seat and look straight ahead. I decided right then I did not like this town, and I wished to transport myself back to the farm, my former church and familiar friends.

I got a phone call at home that afternoon from one of the girls from the Sunday school class who later became my best friend. She asked if I roller-skated. I told her I did but was not very good at it. She invited me to go with their youth group that evening to Club 46 roller rink in Greensburg, Indiana. I decided to give them another chance. I tried my best to stay on my feet, but I took so many falls that my knees were black and blue for days. With each fall I was determined to get up again and keep going. I guess my determination paid off because Don apologized to me for the "bird's nest" remark and thought I was pretty cute. His best friend also thought I was cute and asked for a date. I was only 15; so, I had to get my parents' permission to go on the date. It had to be a double date. I soon discovered that skating was the "in" thing. If you wanted to be part of their group, you skated every Friday and Saturday night and Sunday afternoon and some Sunday nights. I became a very good skater.

Don's best friend and I broke up. I cried until I couldn't cry anymore. I didn't get any sympathy from Don or his girlfriend on the ride home. A few weeks later I met someone else at the roller rink, and we dated for several weeks before breaking up. I asked Don for a ride home from the roller rink that night. After telling him about my breakup and crying my heart out, the next thing I knew he had his arm around my shoulder trying to provide comfort. I wasn't too impressed at the time.

I had been nominated for the Miss Hartsville contest that was held as a moneymaker for the local volunteer fire department. We each had jars with our picture on it with votes being a penny each. Don asked if he could take me to dinner after the results of the contest were announced. I agreed to go with him. I won the contest, much to my surprise but not Don's. He took me to the Bob'O'Link Restaurant in Columbus for dinner. He really treated me like royalty that evening which was very magical. When he brought me home and to the door, I stepped up one step on our porch and turned around. It put me on his level, face to face, and he kissed me goodnight (from that first date when we said goodnight, I stepped up on the first step for our goodbyes). My aunt told me the next day that he had put $50.00 in my jar but didn't want me to know. I promised to keep it a secret. That is when I started to fall in love with him.

We started going "steady" with most of our dates being at the skating rink. We became skating partners, and people still tell us we were good skaters. We had so many good times with other couples and shared many happy memories together.

Since I was still in high school, we spent a lot of time at my house. I had a strict curfew up until the day I was married. If I was not inside the house on time the porch light went on. I made it a point to be home on time so that our last goodbye kiss could be without the porch light. Our closest neighbor was a gossip, and I'm sure she tried to watch from her window even if the porch light was off. We became engaged my senior year of high school and married in June after I graduated. We have been blessed with 43 years together. Has he told me my hair looks like a "bird's nest" lately? I think it was only yesterday. Did he get the drop-dead look? Absolutely!

Special Note: When my husband read this story he said, "That was the best $50.00 investment I ever made!"

It's Time

Well the big day was finally here-my wedding day. As I sat on my bed, I realized this would be the last day spent with my parents as just one of the kids. Everyone was in a "tizzy" as mother would say with one bathroom and six people to get ready for a wedding. I was going to my soon-to-be new home to get ready where I could take as long as needed with no one yelling or rushing me.

I felt a little nauseous; I needed to stay calm. Had I eaten anything today? I couldn't remember. My hands were shaking as I packed. Don't forget the hair dryer. Had I remembered to buy white hose? I told myself not to think about leaving and not to look at my room. My brothers were already fighting over who would take over my room. I didn't want to leave anything important behind. They would probably throw it away. I'd better nail the door shut if I wanted to save those posters on the wall. The wallpaper was so pretty and delicate with its tiny pink roses. I could only imagine what they would do to the walls. The furniture was painted a soft gray. It had belonged to my parents from their early years of marriage. The big closet was stuffed full of childhood treasures, clothes, and now shower and wedding gifts.

Did I forget anything? I'm going to be away two weeks on my honeymoon. No, not two weeks, forever, I'll not be returning. Slowly, go down the stairs, slowly. Don't look back. For goodness sakes, don't cry. How many times had you run up the stairs only to run back down again? How many times had you slammed the door in your brothers' faces and told them to leave you alone? Alone! Why did I feel so alone? Everyone was yelling at everyone else to hurry up. "Did you shine your shoes?" someone asks. "Daddy, make sure the boys wear their ties," I yelled as I headed for the door. "Please, you guys, don't laugh out loud when I say my vows or trip me as I walk down the aisle," I pleaded to my brothers. They wouldn't do that, would they? I felt sick again.

Finally I opened the door to my new home. It was so quiet. I peeked into the spare bedroom. My dress was hanging in its bag with my satin slippers sitting beside it. My long elbow length gloves were waiting nearby. I hoped the veil with the attached tiara stayed on my head. I sensed disaster ahead. The doorbell rang. The bridesmaids were there to get dressed. Everyone was giggling with anticipation. I should have been giggling too, but I was having second thoughts. I wanted to go back home to my room. Had I made a mistake? I didn't want to get married-talk about bride's nerves. Someone asked, "Are you alright?" I was thinking Daddy would kill me after all the money he had spent if I backed out now. I couldn't do that to Daddy!

The doorbell rang again. It was my uncle Clyde. He grabbed me into a big bear hug. He couldn't believe I was getting married. He reached into his pocket and handed me a penny. "Put this in your shoe for good luck," he insisted. I reached down, removed my satin slipper and placed it inside. I had never heard of this tradition, but I smiled and gave him a big hug.

Well, it was time. The music was playing; the songs had been sung. My family was not at the church yet. The minister came in and asked, "Where is your family? It's time to seat your mother." I felt sick again. I explained we only had one bathroom. He paced back and forth looking out the window. He finally spotted our car. Mother's face looked a little pinched. The boys' heads were hanging low. Somebody had been yelled at. They probably all had been lectured. They saw me peeking from around the door. They smiled and waved; I waved back and tried to smile too. Mother was whisked away immediately to take her seat. Daddy came in, took one look at me and started to cry. I grabbed his arm, smiled and whispered, "Please don't cry." I then asked him, "Why were you so late?" "I couldn't get this darned tie right." At least I think those are the words he used. The music became louder; I grabbed onto his arm a little tighter. "Come on Daddy, it's time."

Don and I on our wedding day June 24, 1962

SECTION IV

Where is that young mother who held her babies in her arms, dreaming of the time that she would once again be on her own schedule and not theirs? Memories of her own childhood flooded back as she played in the sand with them. She would race them to the back door, tracking sand onto the floor that she knew would have to be swept up later. Of course, it would have to wait until they had their cookies and milk and big hugs before their afternoon nap. Sometimes she would join them, all snuggled up together in a peaceful sleep.

Egg On Your Face

It was Sunday evening, a week after Easter, and I was cleaning out the refrigerator of the leftovers from Easter dinner. My husband commented that I needed to do something with the eggs that hadn't been colored or used in cooking. I told him, "I don't know what to do with them and don't have the time right now to think about it." Our boys, two and five, were playing nearby waiting for us to come join them on the floor.

We finally got them into bed and went to bed ourselves. Next morning, Don was up and heading into the bathroom when I heard him yelling for me. "You better get in here; I think one of the boys was sick last night." I jumped out of bed and ran to see what he was talking about. I noticed yellow footprints on the rug and on the hallway floor. When entering the bathroom I found yellow, sticky, yucky stuff all over the toilet and floor on each side. It wasn't what Don thought, but what was it? I left the bathroom and followed the footprints into the boys' bedroom which was just a short distance. They were in bed and asleep, but the bottoms of Jon's footed PJ's told the story. Sometime during the night he had apparently gone into the kitchen, taken the eggs out of the refrigerator, carried them into the bathroom and plopped them one by one into the toilet. Some of them, or I should say several of them, didn't make it and slid down the side of the toilet bowl onto the floor. He had stepped and slid in the eggs, tracked them down the hall, climbed into his bed and went back to sleep.

We could not figure out why, or how, without our hearing him. Don had to go to work pleased to get out of clean up duty. I got busy cleaning up the dried egg mess in the bathroom. Due to a very weak stomach, I don't even like to look at cooked eggs in the morning and most definitely not ones sticking to my toilet! I didn't wake the boys choosing to clean the rest of the mess up later. Instead, I tried to piece the puzzle together as to why Jon would throw eggs in the toilet. I finally came to the conclusion that he had heard Don tell me to do something with the eggs and decided to help out. When he woke up that morning he was grinning-talk about egg on your face. I couldn't help but laugh at him. What a mess; what a way to start your day!

Special Note: This is one of those stories I can laugh about now. But at the time, while I was trying to not gag and be sick all over myself, I swore I would never eat another egg!

Things Aren't Always What They Seem

As a young mother of two very active little boys, one of the things I looked forward to was finally getting them tucked into bed and asleep in order to have a little "me" time. It was so relaxing to run a tub of hot water, pour in the bubble bath, even if all I had was the boys' generic brand of bubble bath to soak away the cares of the day.

I had cleaned the bathroom earlier in the day, but the boys then had their bath. Their fishing poles, plastic fish, ducks and boats all lay in the bottom of the tub with the left over bubbles, dirt and sand they had loaded and unloaded with their Tonka trucks. A large pail on the back of the tub for all of their toys was empty. I rinsed the toys and cleaned the tub again! Finally, it was my turn for a good long soak in order to clean the cobwebs from my mind and ease the aches in my body.

I realized it was getting rather late and time to get dried off and into my nightgown and bed. After drying myself, I reached for my powder box with the big fuzzy puff and proceeded to apply the bath powder. I noticed it didn't smell as good as it usually did. Oh well, I was so tired-on with the nightgown and into bed. Don was asleep; so, I carefully got into bed and snuggled up to him and closed my eyes.

I had just settled in when suddenly certain parts of my anatomy felt like they were on fire. I woke my husband, yelling that something was very wrong, and ran for the bathroom. I yanked off my nightgown and discovered my skin was turning a bright red and burning like fire. While looking around the bathroom, I noticed the walls were covered in places with powder. I checked my powder puff realizing to my horror it was full of bathroom cleanser. Quickly I jumped into the shower and starting scrubbing and rinsing. Finally I got the cleanser off and got some relief. Our youngest son Jon, who was two, had watched me clean the bathroom that day. He had gone in and exchanged the powder for the can of cleanser off the back of the commode. I had powdered my body liberally with straight bathroom cleanser.

Wearily I stumbled back into bed to a husband already asleep and oblivious to all that had just transpired. I closed my eyes hoping to get a little sleep before two little boys would again come up with some antic that would make their mother ask herself, "What was I thinking?"

Monkeys on the Bars

Friday evening finally arrived, and I had the weekend off. We looked forward to Friday evenings because the boys and I would pick Don up from work in nearby Columbus. Then we would get chicken dinners to go at Lemley's Cafeteria and take them to Mill Race Park and have a picnic. After eating we would go grocery shopping or to the movies.

I had bathed and dressed the boys allowing them to go outside and wait if they promised not to get dirty again. I stressed to them not to leave the yard. We lived behind the school playground, and they loved to go over and swing in the big swings and play on the monkey bars. I hurriedly finished doing my hair, grabbed my purse and locked the door.

I didn't see the boys anywhere. I yelled for them to hurry, or we would be late picking up daddy. I didn't hear a sound and panicked. My greatest fear as a parent was that someone would snatch my children. I would not leave them alone, even in our yard if I couldn't see them. I ran around to the side of the house and couldn't see them in the schoolyard. With each moment I grew more anxious. I continued to call out their names thinking they must be hiding and playing a joke. While trying to pull my thoughts together, I saw this head come up into view in the back seat of the car. It was Jon who was about 5 at the time. He had tears running down his face and dirt smeared all over it. I ran over to the car and opened the door. He said, "Darrell is killed Mommy." His brother, who was 7, was sitting down on the floorboard of the car with blood pouring from a gash in his head. His clothes were soaked with blood. I ran to the house and got a towel.

They had sneaked over to the monkey bars, and Darrell had hung from his feet and fallen on his head hitting the concrete. They were both crying and apologizing as I was trying to put pressure on the cut while driving out of the driveway and to the hospital. After arriving at the hospital, they took one look at all the blood and dirt and took us right in. Darrell needed several stitches in his head. It suddenly dawned on me that I had forgotten to call Don. When I finally picked him up at work, we decided to get some sandwiches before returning home.

The boys were lectured all the way home on obeying their parents and what happens when they don't. I repeated many times how frightened I was when not being able to find them. Hopefully they had learned their lesson, but so had I. Mine was not to turn my back on two little monkeys, and I whispered a prayer of thanks to God that they were safe.

Our Little Missionary

Our son Jon has a heart of gold and as big as Texas. His friends know they can count on him when in need. As his parents, we have not always understood which drum Jon was listening to while marching through life; but, we could always count on him marching to his own beat.

I stayed home with the boys as a full time mom until Jon went to kindergarten. On the rare occasions they required a babysitter, their grandparents were called upon. Don's mother, "Grandma Dill" as the boys affectionately called her, was the perfect sitter. They would invade her house with gusto, and she would allow them much freedom simply saying–"It's Grandma's house." Our authority was somewhat limited in "Grandma's house!" She took many pictures of their escapades which are now family treasures.

On occasion, if we were going to be gone for several hours to a special event, we would hire a sitter so the boys could supposedly get to bed at a decent hour. After several sitters had tried and failed, we finally found one who was willing to come back the second time–bless her heart. I've never understood why, other than it must have been special training for a future role in God's plan for her life.

During Marcia's first experience as our sitter, Jon tricked her into thinking he had disappeared by hanging from his window by his fingers and toes. After hearing his brother begging her to call the police, he finally made his appearance.

Another incident proved to be quite an expensive one. He did his magic trick of disappearing again. Knowing the first suspected place would be out his window, he climbed into the dryer while closing the door just enough that she couldn't see him. Growing tired of the game he finally appeared again. When turning the dryer on the next day, I got this loud clunking sound that required an immediate visit from the repairman. "I just don't understand how this could have happened ma'am," as he shook his head in puzzlement.

When returning from a Christmas party given by Don's company, we noticed the tree looked slightly askew. Marcia was very apologetic and explained that the boys had accidentally tipped it over, but they had re-decorated it! Things were missing that would never be seen again. The boys blamed our cat, Boots, for that incident.

Our "angel sitter," as she was referred to now, hung in there with us for several years. The boys grew older, and in their words-"babysitter" was for "babies."

Jon had inherited his brother's mo-ped (his brother was now driving) and decided he would get a paper route to make extra spending money. I want to apologize again to all those paper customers who endured paper deliveries in a 4-6 hour time frame, sometimes longer. If someone was watching Jon's favorite show on TV, he might join them; if someone invited him to play ball, the newspaper bag was placed to the side and off he'd go. He had a unique way of stirring up the neighborhood dogs with his mo-ped as well as their owners. After numerous phone calls and his Dad making paper deliveries on many late nights, it was decided that a paper route should probably be delayed to a much later time in his life.

We found out only a few years ago that our son often was at the home of a neighbor cooking dinner for two smaller children whose mother was disabled and very ill. He would cook, wash dishes, vacuum or whatever else needed to be done. He never told us about these missions of mercy. Their daughter shared this story, and we both shed many tears. She told of how her mother spoke of our son as she approached death and what a blessing he had been to her and their family. I was shocked when hearing this. Shock turned to understanding and then pride-pride that only a mother could feel for her child.

I dropped my head in a prayer of thanksgiving saying, "Father you made him with that great big heart, and you gave him the unique beat he marches to. Thank you Father. We survived!"

Special Note: To all of my fellow nursing students (class of 73) that I entertained each day with "Jon stories"-I told you there would be a book someday!

Our "little angels" L. to R. Darrell, Jon

SECTION V

Where is that young nurse who in the prime of her life thought she could be super woman? She thought she could take away the pain and the diseases of the world, one patient at a time. She was wife, mother, and somewhat of a feminist. She wanted it all. Don't try to stop her or tell her she can't do it. It only made her try harder to prove others wrong.

Short Story Twenty-Six

Mom I Need To Talk To You

These words can strike a note of fear in a parent's heart. They can have many meanings-good and bad, happy or sad, everything is OK or not so OK. It's been 25 years since I heard these words, but I can still hear them as if it were yesterday.

It was around 9:00 pm, and I had just gone to bed after a long day of nursing starting at 5:15 am. The boys were on Spring Break. My husband had taken a vacation with the boys, and they had done "guy" things like riding their bikes to a nearby lake and fishing. I had purchased plenty of snacks and root beer for them to take with them. They had just returned home after many good times together. I was almost asleep when our son Darrell, who was 13 at the time, came in and said, "Mom I need to talk to you." I sat up in bed just a little irritated at him for choosing this particular time to have a little talk. I turned the light on. When I saw his face, I knew this was one of those "I'm not OK" moments.

He blurted out that his urine was the color of our closet door, a dark brown. The nurse part of me was at full attention; the mother in me was trying not to show panic. As calmly as I could, I asked when this had started and learned it had been going on for several days. He thought too much root beer had caused the color of his urine to change. I knew this was not possible and began asking him questions. We finally got to the bruise on his left side and the fact that he had been playing basketball with a group of boys in the parking lot at our church. He had tripped and fallen on one of the concrete parking barriers that ran in front of the goal. It caused tremendous pain, but he did not want to appear weak in front of the other boys. He had wanted to cry because it hurt so bad; yet, he had not told anyone about the fall until this moment. After gathering all of the facts I immediately contacted our family doctor. I knew the color of the urine indicated blood. Our doctor was very concerned and advised us to take him in for x-rays the following morning. My husband and I, needless to say, did not sleep much that night. We prayed for our son and asked God to protect him while hoping for something simple. It was a very long night, one of many long nights to come.

We went to the hospital early the next morning, and they ran an ultrasound of the kidney as well as a kidney function test. Our doctor called as soon as he got the results with the news that they had detected a solid mass in Darrell's left kidney. It could be a blood clot from the fall, or the fall itself might suggest a more serious problem. We were very concerned but tried to stay calm and have faith in God. He was taken back into the hospital for more tests which confirmed the original diagnosis of a solid mass in the kidney. These tests took much longer than they would today. Almost five weeks went by before our doctor finally called us into the office with a diagnosis. The bleeding had stopped, but we were advised to keep him very quiet-no contact sports and no school until a specialist saw him. Arrangements were made for Darrell to be admitted to Riley Hospital in Indianapolis, Indiana where a kidney specialist would see him. According to our doctor this specialist was one of the best available. We could not believe this was happening to our son. He was only 13 years old. The past weeks had taken their toll on us. As I went about my nursing duties, I had stopped eating and prayed almost constantly. I had never really fasted before while praying for a specific need. It just seemed the right thing to do; it was instinct. My husband worried that I was not eating and would take me to lunch each day while insisting I drink a milkshake. During that period of time I was never hungry for food. I felt a presence of the Lord and a peace that carried me through the days. I worked as much as possible, not knowing how long I might need to take off to be with my son. The day we left for the hospital was a beautiful sunny day. How could anything be wrong in the world, our world? I remember Darrell getting up front with his Dad because his legs were too long for the backseat. I listened to their small talk and silently prayed, "Dear God, please do not take our child from us." At that moment, I would have given my life for his.

After arriving at the hospital no time was wasted in the testing. He was put in the Teen Cancer Unit, and they had a large room in the center where families all gathered. We became very quickly acquainted with the parents of the other children and the doctors and nurses. He endured many painful procedures for the sake of knowledge. The tests started coming back with good results. If indeed the mass was a tumor, it had not metastasized to the lungs or bones. We rejoiced and thanked God. Down in the parents' lounge the tears started overflowing. We were sitting there one evening, comforting each other and holding hands, when an older man said he had noticed our tears. His granddaughter was there with bone cancer and had to have her leg amputated. He gave us a silver dollar and told us to give it to our boy for good luck.

Darrell had taken his guitar with him. The nurses noticed the guitar and asked him to play for them and some of the other patients. He played John Denver's "Take Me Home, Country Roads" and everyone sang with heavy hearts.

The surgeon came in on our fourth day and advised us that surgery was scheduled in two days. The kidney would be removed. He was sorry, but they couldn't leave a diseased kidney that might take his life. Tests were inconclusive, but they had to use every precaution. I waited anxiously for my husband to come for visitation that evening to tell him what was planned. We made our way to the chapel as we had done almost daily since our arrival. It seemed the large Bible there was always turned to just the scripture needed to encourage us and strengthen our faith in God.

We read the scripture and just held each other and cried. As the tears flowed we prayed, "Lord you gave him to us, and we have loved him and tried to be good parents. But if it is your will to take him, we give him back to you. He is yours." A beautiful presence of God was there, and a complete peace fell over us. We went back to Darrell's room and told him the surgery would be in two days.

During all the tests and the hospitalization, we had many prayer warriors from all over the state praying for our son. Our pastors came on a daily basis, and we prayed continuously for him. He was an excellent patient. I slept on a cot by his bed and kept my hand on his every night praying for a miracle.

The evening before surgery, a woman came into the room and stated they needed to take him through the tunnels to another facility for one last test. She then said, "Mrs. Dillman, you stay here and rest. Your husband and I will take your son over there." As they walked along my husband noticed a pin on her uniform that said, "Try God." She turned around, looked at him, and said, "Mr. Dillman, your boy is going to be OK." A feeling of total peace swept over my husband. The procedure was a needle biopsy that could further track the cancer in his body. It was a risky test, and we had to sign papers releasing them from all responsibility. We prayed that it was the right decision. He was scheduled for surgery the next morning. We didn't sleep much that night and talked for several hours.

When morning came our pastors had prayer. The nurses came in and prepped him for surgery. They had done everything but the pre-op injection. We were standing around his bed talking and waiting when the door opened and several doctors entered. The surgeon came over, slapped him on the rear, and told him to get out of that bed and get dressed to go home. He could not explain it, but the needle biopsy showed the mass was not a malignant tumor after all but a water filled cyst. It was very rare for a 13-year-old boy to have such a cyst; they usually occurred in elderly men. It took Darrell about two minutes to get the gown off and the pants on. He came out of the bathroom and said, "Let's get out of here. I want a cheeseburger." We joined hands with our pastors and prayed a prayer of thanksgiving for our miracle as the doctors looked on with smiles. This was a glorious day for all of us!

It took only minutes to sign the proper papers and to set up a follow up visit with the doctor. At the time his surgery was to have taken place we were sitting in Bob Evans eating breakfast. Darrell had two cheeseburgers and a double order of fries. He sure made up for all the food missed!

We then realized everyone was praying at that moment thinking Darrell was in surgery. We decided to stop at a few of our friends' homes and let him share the good news. The look on their faces was priceless. He bounced out of the car and up to the door and back again smiling ear to ear.

Was it a miracle? My husband confided later that he was sure the lady who came to get our son for that last test was an angel. She had an aura around her, and the peace that came over him was life changing. He cannot talk about it even now without the tears flowing.

Special Note: Our son is now 40 years old and married with two beautiful children who are the lights of our life. A few years ago he developed nephritis and had some kidney tests done. The technician asked him if he had had surgery on his left kidney. He explained that he'd had a problem as a child. The technician told him that there was a nub of flesh there that looked like a dried up grape. Well, we knew there had not been surgery on his kidney other than the surgery done by the Great Physician. Oh, how good God is to His children! We praise Him and thank Him for all He has done for us. This was a landmark in our lives that we have returned to time after time during trouble to strengthen our faith and to reassure us that God is in control.

He Made A Way Of Escape

It was a cold January day in l976. I had just finished my day shift nursing job and was feeling a bit down. It was Friday, my last day of work for approximately six weeks. I was scheduled for gall bladder surgery on Monday and had mixed feelings about this surgery. I would be glad to be free of the pain and nausea but dreaded having to go through the surgery. I had put it off for four years and had not felt well for several months.

I rode to work each day with two ladies who worked at a nearby factory. One of the ladies just lived down the street, and it worked out well for all of us to ride together. I climbed into the back seat of the car, and we all agreed it was good to be going home after a rough week at work to enjoy a quiet weekend.

We drove the short distance from the nursing facility where I worked onto the highway. After driving only a short distance, the driver of our car looked back and commented on the closeness of the car behind us. I suddenly had cold chills, and the hair on my body stood up. I had this unexplainable urge to scoot down in my seat feeling as if a gun was pointed at my head. I could hardly breathe; I was so frightened. Just as I started to say something to the others, the car following us quickly pulled to the side of our car. It was then I looked up into the most evil face I had ever seen.

The face belonged to a young person. I couldn't tell if it was the face of a male or female. Their hair was short and messy. They were wearing a white shirt with no coat. The window was down, and they were yelling obscenities. Their arm was resting on the edge of the window while the other hand balanced a large pistol pointed at the head of my friend who was driving. They yelled that we were going to die. The driver was laughing and kept his speed the same as our car. We could not get in front or behind him. I told my friend not to look at them but to keep looking straight ahead while driving her best. My other friend and I started praying while trying to figure out our next step. We knew the gun could go off at any moment, and our driver could be dead and our car out of control. A car finally came down the highway on their side, and we saw them speed ahead and pull off the road only to get behind us and then beside us again. The threats continued. This happened several times, and we knew we had to do something. We prayed together–"Oh God, help us. We don't want to die here on the highway like this. Please God, show us what to do." I knew what we needed to do, but it would take all the courage we could muster. We didn't have much time to think about it. Our escape was just ahead.

Two weeks prior to this incident, my husband and our two small boys picked me up from my nursing job around midnight on Saturday. I always worked the 3-pm-11-pm shifts on weekends in order to attend church on Sunday morning. It was a really nasty night with a lot of snow. He decided he would take me to work and then pick me up. We lived about sixteen miles from my work place. We were about five miles from our home when a tire went flat. He got out of the car and tried to loosen the lug nuts on the wheel, but they wouldn't budge. He tried for quite a long time until realizing we needed help. It was well past midnight. Our boys were asleep in the backseat oblivious to our situation.

There was a house across the road. He told me to sit tight, and he would see if someone at the house could help us. He knocked on the door. A man came, and my husband explained our situation. He asked my husband to step inside while he got his coat. Then he helped Don change the tire. After they got the tire changed, he asked him to come inside and wash his hands. Don noticed a note pad on the desk of their home. He picked it up and wrote Matthew 25:40-"Inasmuch as ye have done it unto one of the least of these my brethren, ye have done it unto me." The man read the note and shared he too was a Christian and drove their church bus every Sunday morning. Don then told him I was a nurse and traveled this highway every day, and he was thankful I had not been by myself with a flat tire. He told Don that if I ever needed their help for anything to feel free to stop. We drove on home that night with thankful hearts. Our flat tire had happened in front of this welcoming home, not miles away where my husband would have had to walk for help or wait for someone to come along to help us. My husband shared about their conversation and the offer of the man to be of assistance if ever needed.

Now we were quickly approaching this same house, and I told the ladies of my plan. I knew God was directing me. We were in a two-door car. I was in the back. Timing was everything. The house was just ahead. I told the driver to somehow get ahead of the pursuing car and pull quickly in front of the house and let me out to run up, knock on the door and identify myself. There was no time to think about being afraid or possibly being gunned down. We made our move and slammed on the brakes in front of the house. I jumped out of the car and ran to the door and pounded on it. The woman, who had never met me, came to the door with a small baby in her arms. I yelled, "I am Rena Dillman, the lady who had the flat tire in front of your home, and we are being chased and threatened with a gun. She motioned for us to come inside, then slammed and quickly shut and locked the door. The young people in the car watched us as we all ran inside. They did a U turn and revved their engine trying to decide, I'm sure, what to do next.

We asked her to call the police as quickly as she could while shaking so badly we could hardly talk. It seemed like only a few minutes passed before the sheriff's officers arrived. We recounted our story and described the vehicle as well as the two young people. We were told to stay put until they apprehended them. A sheriff's deputy stayed with us. In a matter of minutes they had them in custody. They were on their way to jail, and we were free to go. We couldn't thank this compassionate woman enough. We were all still in shock. We opened the door and walked out. One of the ladies said, "Look at the sky. Isn't that just about the most beautiful thing you've ever seen?" The sun had curiously peered its face through the clouds as if God was telling us we would be OK. We were all just in awe of its beauty. It was like God was smiling at us. It had a calming and peaceful effect as we drove home.

Of course, they wanted to know how in the world I knew to stop at that house. There had been no time to explain our previous encounter with these wonderful people. It was like a bad dream, and we were trying to figure it all out. We pulled up in front of my house, and I went inside. The realization of what just happened hit. I started to shake uncontrollably. My children were still at the babysitters, and I was alone. I called my husband's office and asked his secretary if I could please speak to him. When he got on the phone all I could say was, "Can you please come home, NOW?" When he got home, all I could say was, "Just hold me." I finally got the story out but shook for hours. Fear had taken over, and I was convinced these people were after our family and would be coming at any time. My husband called the sheriff's department, and they assured us that they were in custody. The gun was not a real gun but an air pistol. The sheriff said it looked so real that had they pointed it at him he would have fired back. They were 16 and 14 years old, had skipped school and were drunk and high on drugs. They had picked us out for a little fun. He assured us again that we were safe. The court declared that since they were juveniles we would need to determine whether or not to press charges. We chose not to. They were ordered to get counseling, and we prayed for their needs.

I checked into the hospital. Gallbladder surgery was not nearly as scary as having a gun pointed at your head. I had a lot of time to think about what had happened that day while recuperating. I was overwhelmed by it all. God had provided a way of escape before I even needed it. He had given me a safe house and caring people by way of a flat tire on a snowy January night. He had moved upon my husband to take me to work instead of personally driving the car and being alone. I doubt if I would have gone up to that door alone. God had given a way for us even when we were unaware of his providence. This was a life changing experience for all of us. Why did this happen? I've asked myself that so many times. I've wondered on many occasions what happened to the two young people who had terrorized us that day. I truly believe our steps are ordered of the Lord, and He walks with us each and every step of the way.

Special Note: Shirley, the driver of our car, recently died after serving the community of Hope in many wonderful ways. I have vivid memories of her driving down the highway with the car radio blasting her favorite country songs. She would sing along and pound out the rhythm on the steering wheel while I would sit in the back seat thinking no one should be that energetic at 6:00 am. When remembering her, I see this great big smile as if the happiness inside her just had to burst forth. Like the other passenger Euna, I am not a morning person. It took awhile for our smiles to break forth and be a blessing to others. By sharing her exuberance for life, Shirley always made sure we eventually had smiles on our faces. I miss those smiles!

Paints and Brushes

I'd like to share how I got into the world of paints and brushes. I got married! My husband Don and I received an oil painting for a wedding gift. A Jennings County artist, a friend of Don's parents, help coordinate the wedding and did the painting.

I was so impressed and excited about having a real oil painting in our new home that I made a nuisance of myself to the giver of the gift. I asked so many questions about how it was done that she finally agreed to share her talents. Once a week I traveled to her home for lessons that cost $1.50 for two hours, and she furnished everything! I did this for almost two years.

Being newly married, we had very little extra money for lessons and art supplies. My husband surprised me our first Christmas together with a metal paint box filled with paints and brushes and a wooden easel. I was ecstatic about having my own supplies enabling me to paint at home.

Our older son Darrell came along two years later, and my painting time was really cut short. By the time our second son Jon arrived I was not painting at all. My paints were stuck back in a closet but not forgotten.

As my sons became school age, I had more time on my hands and volunteered at a children's clinic in nearby Columbus, Indiana. My coworkers at the clinic encouraged me to go to nursing school. When my youngest started kindergarten, I started in the Practical Nursing Program. With my husband's encouragement and his great sacrifice of time, I graduated with flying colors.

For the next eleven years I gave my full attention to my family and my nursing career. I painted only on rare occasions for a special gift or for my family. This all changed when realizing I was trying to be "super woman." I was working full time, sometimes six days a week, while attending school two days a week striving to earn an RN degree. In addition, I was trying to keep up my home and be a good mother and wife. After two years of this routine, I finally realized "super woman" is for the movies-not real life.

I resigned my nursing job and left school after finishing the semester. For three months, I stayed home trying to figure out who I was and where I wanted to go with my life. After this short leave I felt it was time to go back to work part-time. I took a job at a local nursing facility, and it was there I discovered my God given talent.

I was asked to donate a painting for the heart fund auction to be held at the nursing facility. When my coworkers saw the painting they asked if I would be willing to teach them to paint. I agreed to help them to the best of my ability. My first painting class was held in the dining room of the facility with six students. Shortly after beginning this class, the owner of a local art and frame shop in Hope asked me to teach in her shop. She also offered to teach me what she had learned through the years as well. I was an eager student and teacher. I was back to juggling two careers and a home again. I did this for eighteen months before realizing I had to make a choice. I chose art.

I've never regretted that decision. I have been teaching art for 24 years now. I'm helping people realize their dreams of being an artist. It is quite satisfying to watch them go out of the studio with their finished paintings and smiles on their faces. I have learned so much from them. Not only are they my students, they also have become good friends and prayer partners. Edna Bergman, 84 and Ruth Harker, 82, have enriched my life tremendously with their life stories. They each began art classes at the age of 79. My youngest beginning student was 4 years old and my oldest 91 years young. God has certainly blessed me!

Special Note: I want to express much appreciation to Dennis and Patty Schulz who have been great friends. They have generously provided studio space and monetary support in our endeavors at the Art Guild of Hope.

SECTION VI

Where is that middle-aged artist? She has grown somewhat wiser. She is following her heart now. Life is not so simple. Babies become adults. They make their own lives. That young man she thought would never want to be a moment away from her is engrossed in his work and outside interests. She paints pictures; she teaches others to paint pictures. A whole new world is opened up to her through art. She meets new people, special people, sent from God to share with her His perfect plan for her life.

The Gift

Power, comfort, wisdom, strength, compassion, love, deliverance, healing, protection, conviction, joy, discernment. These words, these feelings come to my mind as I think about the difference The Holy Ghost has made in my life.

I received the Baptism of the Holy Ghost July 27, 1984 in a revival meeting with Reverend Charles Wilks in North Vernon, Indiana. He had preached on the rapture of the church, and I had never seen or heard anything quite like it. Reluctantly I attended this service due to a series of events in my own life suggesting a need for a change.

Reverend Tony Carson was the pastor of the church, and I had met him and his wife Martha in December of 1983 when they visited the Gold Nugget Pawn Shop. They had seen an ad in the newspaper advertising snow skis. I had recently opened a retail art business and painting studio in the rear of the store. During the week I taught several art classes and sold supplies and crafts. A large wall featured several of my paintings for sale. I was working in the retail section of my shop when noticing them looking at the paintings. They asked if I had done the paintings. We started talking, and I noticed their matching jackets which had "Apostolic Christian Academy" on the back. They explained that it was a Christian school that was part of their church. We continued to talk about art, and they signed up for art classes before leaving. The feeling I had while talking to them, of wanting to cry but not knowing why, was one that would change my life forever. The Holy Ghost was at work!

In a couple of weeks Martha Carson came to painting class. While walking over to the Heritage House Restaurant we shared about our families. I informed her of some health problems and my impending surgery and asked for prayer. I really felt at ease talking to her, and she seemed to genuinely care. She continued to come to classes, and Reverend Carson came for a class taught by another teacher, Debbie Hatton. While completing some paper work during Debbie's class one day, he invited me to their church the following Sunday. I told him I would if physically able. At this point I was very ill and surgery was only a few days away. I was very fearful and uncertain of the outcome. I had been in church my whole life and trusted God; however, I had felt for a long time there was something missing- a void. I didn't know what it was nor how to fill it. I had even counseled with my pastor. Now The Holy Ghost was really at work.

The pawnshop owner's wife Alta and I had many discussions about church and the baptism of the Holy Ghost. As I was leaving the next day, she asked how I was feeling and the exact time of my surgery and if I had been anointed and prayed for. I didn't know anyone who provided such a service. Suddenly I remembered Reverend Carson, the Apostolic preacher. I mentioned the invitation.

When Sunday rolled around, I was really nervous about going to an unfamiliar church and had no idea what to expect. We headed for the nearby town of North Vernon which took 45 minutes instead of 30 minutes as we thought. As soon as we pulled into the church parking lot and got out of the car, we could hear the music playing from inside the church. I felt a little faint and asked the Lord, "What have I gotten myself into?" It took all my courage to walk into that building. To make matters even worse, when we walked in, the people were all up walking around with this loud music playing. They were greeting one another, but I had never seen people walking around so much. I panicked! I had no idea what to do or where to sit. Reverend Carson saw us and came down and found us seats. I was petrified—questioning why I had put us into this situation. After everyone sat down the atmosphere changed. I can still remember that service, as it will forever be an indelible image in my mind. "Thanks to Calvary" was the special, and several people testified. My husband and I sat there and cried with tears flowing down our faces. I didn't know why I was crying, but I couldn't stop. The Holy Ghost was at work.

People were moving up to the altar and forming a line across the front of the church. Initially I didn't know it was a prayer line. I wanted to be prayed for but couldn't make my body move from the chair. My friend punched me and said, "Rena go up there." I just couldn't go by myself. She took my hand and led me to the altar. Reverend Carson placed oil on my forehead and prayed a prayer for healing. I felt warmth permeate my body, especially in my mid section. I was overwhelmed with peace while returning to my seat and cried through most of the service. From the first moment of entering the building I felt the tangible presence of God. This was the first time I had truly felt The Holy Ghost at work in my own life.

I had the surgery and everything went exceptionally well other than being informed I needed three units of blood. Even though I was a nurse and certainly believed in blood transfusions, I felt deep in my heart God was intervening for reasons unknown. I asked several people to pray that my blood count would come up on its own. The Lord worked a miracle. My blood count improved without the transfusions. The Holy Ghost was definitely at work.

I spent four days in the hospital. During that time, I was overwhelmed with joy and thanksgiving for what God had done. I lifted my hands in praise because it felt right. Reverend Carson visited and asked me to share my testimony in their church. Of course I did and then attended a few more times. I was very torn between my old church and this new church experience.

My brother Ron, who had an alcohol problem, was going through tremendous problems in his life. He was living with our parents after losing his family through divorce. My parents were unable to cope with his depression and sorrow. My mother called to ask for my help. Reverend Carson came to my mind. I called him, and he said he would be glad to talk to him. They were having revival services.

In a few hours after dropping him off at the church, I received a phone call from Ron. He excitedly told me he was going to be baptized in the name of Jesus that night and requested my presence for this momentous occasion. I called a friend and asked her if she would go. While walking into that service, I felt such a presence of God that the hair on my body stood straight up. Reverend Wilks was like no other preacher I had ever heard. He preached on the rapture, and I thought and felt like I was going to be right there. At the end of the service, my brother went forward for prayer and then to prepare for baptism. Reverend Carson motioned for me to come forward. While standing there, I watched and heard my brother receive the baptism of the Holy Ghost and then speak in tongues while lifted from the water. Reverend Wilks leaned over and said, "I can tell by your face you would like to receive the Holy Ghost like your brother." I nodded my head. He laid his hand on my head, and I too received the baptism of the Holy Ghost and spoke in tongues. From that moment, I could no longer deny, the void which I had felt for so long was now filled. Ron and I received a precious gift, the most precious gift of the Holy Ghost. John 3:8 states-"The wind bloweth where it listeth, and thou hearest the sound thereof, but canst not tell whence it cometh, and whither it goeth: so is every one that is born of the Spirit."

I've written this account of receiving the Holy Ghost for my children and grandchildren so they might know and share the most wonderful experience of my life. For you see it has changed me; it has made me who I am today. The mother and grandmother you know is most definitely not the same person I used to be. The old me doesn't live here anymore. It is my prayer and always will be that you too receive this gift of the Holy Ghost according to Acts 2:38-39. Then Peter said unto them, "Repent, and be baptized every one of you in the name of Jesus Christ for the remission of sins, and ye shall receive the gift of the Holy Ghost. For the promise is unto you, and to your children, and to all that are afar off, even as many as the Lord our God shall call." Praise God!!

Yes, Lord, I'll Be Baptized In Your Name

As I sat listening to the sermon being preached, I felt a stirring in my heart to obey the voice of God that continued to resound in my head. For many weeks I had been listening to that voice. I had tried to reason with the One whose voice I had heard. Just two months before I had received the Holy Ghost. Constantly I talked to the Lord-"Lord, I've already been baptized. Why would I need to be re-baptized? Wouldn't that be offensive to you? I have never felt exactly right about my first baptism, but I don't know if it is you I'm listening to or myself." My mind kept drifting back to the first experience.

I was only five years old when baptized the first time, and I didn't feel good about it. The minister lost his grip when he brought me up and was slow in finding me in the water. I panicked and came up like a missile. Everyone in the auditorium thought it was funny and laughed. I didn't think it was at all funny. I almost drowned on the day of my baptism.

I kept thinking of the scriptures-Acts 2:38, "Repent, and be baptized every one of you in the name of Jesus Christ for the remission of sins, and ye shall receive the gift of the Holy Ghost;" and, Mark 16:16, "He that believeth and is baptized shall be saved; but he that believeth not shall be damned." I was feeling very uncomfortable. I felt a tug at my heart. Reverend Carson kept preaching. He was talking about obedience with tears flowing down his face. "Yes Lord, I'll be baptized in your name," I heard him say. I knew what I needed to do but first needed to ask Reverend Carson a few questions. I sat in my seat during the altar call which was quite lengthy. He continued to extend the call and was on his face praying behind the pulpit. In my heart I knew he was praying for me.

After the service ended, I asked Reverend Carson if I could talk to him. My defensive side asked many questions about his sermon. Was he talking about me? The tears were starting up again. My heart was pounding. I had come to a crossroads with no turning back. Today was the day; I had to obey the voice of God. My brother Ron was with me, and he was grinning because he knew I had finally come to the realization that I needed to be baptized in the name of Jesus. We decided to go get a sandwich and then return for the baptism. I was too excited to eat much. Now that I had made my decision, I wanted to get it done.

Reverend Carson and his wife Martha, their children Rachael and David, my brother Ron and I gathered for my baptism. The baptismal was a horse trough behind the pulpit, and the water was freezing. When I stepped into the water, it became unexplainably warm. I went down into the water one person and came up another. I felt love like never before and forgave those that I had harbored unforgiveness in my heart for years. A thousand pounds seemingly came off my back. The sins I had carried for all those years were remitted, left behind in that water trough. I felt so light.

After I dressed and came out everyone said I looked different-that my countenance was changed. I felt so warm and glowing, as if I was floating a little bit above the floor. This feeling lasted three days. I had the sudden realization of now being rapture ready.

This was an assurance never experienced before- if I would die at that moment or the Lord came for me, I would be ready. Reverend Carson said I had to come to this awareness for myself. I told him that this was what I had been hungering and thirsting for but had not known it. Not only was my void filled, I was overflowing with completeness. When walking down the street and looking at people passing by, I expected them to stop and ask what had happened and to tell me they could see the changes.

In as much as I wanted people to recognize these changes, I also wanted them to understand. Instead, it created some confusion. In retrospect I certainly can understand. In all likelihood I would have reacted similarly if things were reversed. As it often does, time helps to clarify such situations. I wish to take this opportunity twenty years later to express how much I love my family and others more than I ever could have without this experience. It is my sincere hope the love shown you these past years has been the Christ kind of love flowing through me. Truly, God has blessed me through my family and the many friends He has brought into my life to share this wonderful experience.

I also want to take this opportunity to thank Reverend Carson and his wife Martha for sharing this gospel, for mentoring and pastoring, and for being the very best friends that God could have possibly given.

My prayer is again and always will be that my family and friends will hear and obey this Acts 2:38 message. I have given this account of my baptism experience so that it might help someone to say, "Yes, Lord, I will be baptized in your name."

Cassie

Cassie was an old woman, at least she seemed old. However, she couldn't have been as old as I thought because she passed away only a few years ago.

I remember her so well. I must have been around five when I first became aware that Cassie was different from the others in our church. She was different in the way she worshipped. When the preacher said something that she agreed wholeheartedly with, she would rise from her pew with both hands in the air waving a hanky while shouting, "Praise the Lord." Sometimes this was accompanied by tears flowing freely down her cheeks or quiet laughter. I was absolutely intrigued by this woman and a little frightened as well.

I can still hear my dad's comments on many occasions as he drove us home from church. "I just don't understand why she doesn't go to the Holy Roller church down the street instead of our Baptist church."

Years passed by, and I still felt a stirring inside every time Cassie would shout. I never talked about it to anyone, not even my parents. My father took a job in another town, and we were moving. I was 14 and felt as if a very precious part of my life was being left behind. I would miss our church-the one where I had felt the Lord tugging at my heart, the one which I was baptized in at a very young age. It was hard to leave my friends, my church and Cassie.

There was not a Baptist Church in our small town. My mother prayed. In two weeks time, a Baptist minister came to our door and asked if we would be interested in a Baptist Home Mission Church. Mother was a woman of great faith, and she knew immediately this was the answer to her prayers. Our family of six and the minister's family started the church in an old abandoned church building. I was a young teenager, and it was hard going to a church with only my siblings and the minister's small children. But God blessed this church as it grew.

The years passed. I met my husband, and we were married in that little church. Later our sons were dedicated to the Lord there. When the boys were four and seven we moved and went to another Baptist church. Cassie was not in my thoughts for many, many years. My life was so full and so busy.

I was approaching 40 years of age when realizing there was a huge void in my heart. It had been there for a long time. I knew God and trusted Him to lead me in the direction He wanted me to go. He knew the desires of my heart and how much I wanted a deeper relationship with Him. Once again, He answered my prayers and sent some very special people into my life who became and still remain treasured friends. Through their friendship and God's direction, I was baptized again and became Pentecostal. It was what I had been hungering and thirsting for in my soul. I was filled to overflowing with the Spirit of Christ, joy, peace and happiness. I now felt this wonderful freedom to express my praise and worship in church.

One day a vision of Cassie came to my mind. I said, "Lord, now I know what she was shouting about." I thought about her all the time and felt an urgency to contact her. I wondered if she could possibly still be living. I wanted so badly to let her know what an impact she had had on my life as a child. Now, I too was able to shout and stand and say out loud, "Praise the Lord" as I cried out to the Lord from the depths of my soul.

When I visited my parents the next week, I asked if they remembered her and if she was still living. I was so pleased to hear she was and lived only a short distance away. I got her address and wrote about what had been in my heart these many years and about the major changes in my life–I was so happy. Within a few days, I received a letter back from her and a poem that she had written about the Lord. I was so thankful that God had provided the opportunity to thank Cassie. She had made such a difference in my life through her example of praise and worship while ignoring the giggles of the children and the stares and whispers of the adults.

God used this wonderful lady to touch a little girl's life, and I'd like to think He used that little girl to touch a dear elderly lady's life. Thank you Lord for giving us the desires of our hearts.

The Encounter

It was a cold, dreary, dark day; and, I was lost in what I was doing at the moment. I was at my studio at the rear of the Gold Nugget Pawn Shop. The door was closed that connected my studio to the rest of the building, and I was happily painting away. I was as content as could be. I was sitting at a table placed directly under a skylight in order to get as much natural light as possible. I loved to paint in this studio because it was so quiet and peaceful; yet, outside my door there was always a flourish of activity going on. Occasionally, I would look up to see a man with a rifle or shotgun testing it out by sighting it in my direction. They seemed to target my paintings. There were always musical instruments, stereo and sound equipment coming in and going out, people coming and going throughout the day bringing in their treasures to pawn and people looking for new treasures and bargains. It had been a very quiet day.

I had been painting for a few hours and almost had a painting of a mother and child finished when I heard the door open. I looked up to see that a man had entered the room. I didn't pay close attention to him at first because of being busy with my painting. He walked around the room and eventually stood beside me and watched the strokes of my brush. He finally spoke and said, "You paint with so much love." I thanked him, and he continued to stand there for a few moments.

I started to feel uncomfortable and got up from my chair and walked over close to the door by the sink where we washed our brushes. The thought went through my head that I was near enough to the door that I could get the attention of the man who worked in the pawnshop if needed. I felt compelled to say something to the man as he continued to stand and look at the painting and asked him where he was from. He said, "I use to be from a small town near here." He seemed to have something he wanted to say. I got a better look as I was talking to him. He was dressed very oddly. I noticed his clothes seemed to be many years old. He had a blue knit cap pulled down over his head. He was wearing old pants that were thin and a green army surplus coat. I noticed his shoes were old blue canvas. He had red-rimmed eyes and a stubble of a beard.

I asked him where home was now, and he started walking toward the door. He said, "I'm getting ready to go home to the gospel of Jesus Christ." I made eye contact with him, and he walked out the door and disappeared. I stood there for a moment and then went out and asked the man who worked in the pawnshop where the man was that just left my studio. He said he hadn't seen a man enter or leave the studio. We both went out to the street and looked around, but there was no one in sight. I felt so strange as if I had only imagined this encounter. The man in charge of the pawnshop just shook his head and went on with his work. I went back to my studio and thought about what had just transpired. I just sat there, and the thought came to me that I had just been in the presence of an angel. I didn't feel any fear now. There had to be some meaning to what had just happened. I couldn't make any sense out of it. If it was an angel, I should have asked him more questions, been friendlier and listened more intently. Had he come to bring a message that I didn't get? Did he sense I was not ready for what he had to say? I will always wonder if I missed something life changing that day. I wish I had offered him a cold bottle of pop or asked him to sit down for a while. The Bible tells us in Hebrews 13: 2, "Be not forgetful to entertain strangers: for thereby some have entertained angels unawares."

Little Churches

It was 1984, and I had just embarked on a new business venture. I opened a painting studio and retail business in my hometown of Hope, Indiana in the rear of the Gold Nugget Pawn Shop. My business grew. On the advice of my dad, I opened another studio and retail business in Metamora, Indiana-a historical site located near the farm where I grew up. It was exciting being back in my old childhood hometown with family and friends. I decided to meet with a local artist Mark Day, and discuss the possibility of forming a partnership. Mark and I elected to rent a house behind the gristmill in Metamora and open up a studio that would mostly feature our original art works.

Mark had an old Ford Pinto station wagon which he had stacked to the very top with his art pieces. He came and picked me up early one morning, and we squeezed in a few more of my things and headed out for the hour-long drive to Metamora. I had not had time for breakfast; so, I asked him if we could stop in Greensburg, Indiana for a McMuffin at McDonalds. On our way there his car's engine started making funny noises. I didn't say anything, but I could tell he was concerned. He wanted to stop and put some oil in the car when we got to Greensburg. Since we couldn't find anything open to buy oil, we headed to the drive-up at McDonald's for breakfast.

It is my routine to pray for my food before I eat. I bowed my head and silently blessed my food and thanked God we had made it this far. While praying, I reached up and just laid my hand on the dash of the car and again silently prayed that God would touch this car and heal the problem. I then asked God to do it in such a way that Mark would know that it was He who had touched the car. Then I started eating, and we were on our way again. Mark said he thought we would just go ahead and try to make it since nothing was open yet to buy oil. We got out on the road and no noise. The car was purring like a kitten. Mark was silent for a while. Then he said, "I noticed you prayed for your food back there. You prayed for this car too, didn't you?" I told him God had answered my prayer. He shook his head, laughed and said that his car hadn't run that well in years. We drove on without another problem with the car and back home again that evening.

I didn't think about that trip again for quite awhile, but word got back that Mark had told someone that if they had car problems to come see me. I was better than a mechanic.

We were partners for about two years, and then I took over the shop on my own. I ran into Mark a few years later and asked him if he still had that old Ford Pinto. He shook his head and laughed. He hadn't had any more problems with that car, and his daughter had driven it all through high school!

This reminds me of how much God cares for us. A simple, very sincere prayer was whispered in faith that day to demonstrate the love of God to a friend who sometimes laughed at my religious notions. It was shortly after this experience that Mark started putting small churches in his landscapes. He told me those little churches were for me. I also think those little churches are thank you notes to God.

Let Him Go Ma'am

The tears were stinging the back of my eyes, threatening to spill over, as I drove along the highway fighting the lump in my throat. "Oh God, I prayed silently, what am I doing? Why do I have to be the one to make this trip? I don't agree with this Lord; you know I tried to talk them out of it. Please Lord, don't let anything happen to our son."

I snuck a peek out of the corner of my eye at my 16-year-old son Darrell who was sitting next to me in the car. He had become so tall and quiet. His curly blond hair blew wildly in the wind, and his piercing blue eyes looked straight ahead as they danced with excitement.

"How could I have let them talk me into this?" My husband and son had been convincing me for days that it was a good deal, a bargain in fact. Ever since the day they saw the ad in the paper, "Honda Motorcycle For Sale-In Excellent Condition," they had been wearing me down.

At that time Darrell had a part-time job at a local steak house. He and his Dad thought it would be much more economical for him to ride the cycle to work than to drive the car. They decided to go check the Honda out. They liked what they saw, and they made an offer which was subsequently accepted.

As my son and I headed down the highway so he could pick up the cycle and ride it home, I didn't like what I felt at all. I didn't like being a part of this dangerous scenario, but I had no control over the events that were taking place. This was the way I felt when he got the mo-ped when he was 14 and the air rifle at age 12. His father and I were not on good terms over the air rifle for a long time. Fortunately he had done OK with it-no injuries to himself or anyone else. It was now in the back of his closet somewhere long forgotten. The mo-ped had been passed down to his younger brother Jon.

"Here we are Mom," I heard him say. "Just pull in there behind the cycle. Isn't it a beauty? It's really in good shape isn't it?" He jumped out of the car and went over to the owner and shook his hand. "How're you doing?" he asked. "My Mom brought me in to pick up my cycle."

I got out of the car; tears were welling up in my eyes. The owner, an older man, walked over, and he looked at me and sensed that I was having problems with this. "Your boy's going to be just fine," he said. "I've talked to him and given him some good advice. I've ridden motorcycles my whole life, and I have never had an accident ma'am. I watched your boy try it out. He knows what he's doing."

I looked into his eyes and then at my son sitting on the motorcycle waiting to take off. You could see the excitement and the anticipation on his face. "Let him go ma'am," I heard the man say to me, "Let your boy go."

I got back into my car and watched him turn the key and rev the engine. I nodded my head, and he took off. In a blink of an eye my son was gone. I looked at the man; he was smiling at me. I smiled back, started my car and drove off in a different direction on my way back home. "Let him go ma'am," I heard him say over and over in my head. "I just did," I whispered as I let the tears flow freely. "I just did."

I've Met The Girl I'm Going To Marry

It was getting really late and our son Darrell was not yet home. He was in college now but still living at home and commuting to school each day. It was unusual for him to be out late without telling us beforehand. The clock said 2:30 am, and I had not gone to sleep yet. I was worried that something had happened to our son. I woke my husband expressing concerns that Darrell was not yet home. We agreed that something must be wrong, or he would have called us. Don decided to get up and go downtown, out to the school and around to some of his friends' houses to see if his car was there. I got up and sat in a chair in the living room praying that he was OK.

A few minutes later Don came home. Of course I was anxious to hear the details. Darrell had driven down to the town square where sometimes the teens would gather and talk. At this hour in the morning, we were surprised to find that he was parked on the town square but was not alone. Don said he was with a girl, and they were sitting in Darrell's car talking. We just sat there and looked at each other trying to figure out what was going on with our son. This was so out of character for him to fail to tell us that he would be out so late. I think the reality of our son's growing up and away from us was finally sinking in. We didn't like this feeling at all.

Darrell came home shortly after Don. I'm sure the humiliation of having his father driving around the town square at 2:30 in the morning looking his way was enough to convince him to head home. He came in with a silly grin on his face. Before I could say a word he said, "I've met the girl I'm going to marry Mom." I can only imagine the expression on my face. I think for the first time in my life I was totally speechless. I can't remember saying anything. Don asked him when we were going to meet her. He said he was bringing her to our home the next evening. Finally we all went to bed, but I don't think Don and I got much sleep that night. I kept him awake for hours asking questions like, "What did she look like, who is she, where does she live, who are her parents, where did he meet her?" His answer was, "I really couldn't tell you; it was dark." I lay there wondering about this individual who was sleeping in our boy's bed reluctantly realizing he was now a man.

When morning came and we had the opportunity to talk to Darrell, he answered a few of our questions. He didn't seem to have the answers to all the important ones. We did find out they had met at the ballgame in town, and she previously had dated a friend of his.

After what seemed like the longest day in history, they pulled into our driveway. They entered hand in hand. They sat down on the sofa together, and she giggled. I sat in the chair closest to them, and I started asking her questions about herself and her family. Dana likes to call it "The Interrogation Process" and rightly so. I was firing questions as fast as she could answer them. I got my answers and a lot of nervous giggles. From the first moment we met she endeared herself to us. They were inseparable from that time on. They were married two years later, and she has been the daughter that we had always wanted. She has embraced our family, even with all our "warts," and has given us two beautiful grandchildren, Blake now 16 and Jessica 13. We have likewise embraced her family. We are truly blessed for they have added so much joy to our lives.

Special Note: Dana, I'm so glad you haven't held the "interrogation" against me. I'll be happy to be there if needed when Blake and Jessica come home and say, "I've met the person I'm going to marry Mom."

Happy Mother's Day!

He Gives Us The Desires Of Our Heart

What a night! I was shaking, and my knees were weak. I had just spent the past hour trying to keep a child alive until the ambulance could get there to transport him to the emergency room. I made my way toward the break room. It would be a short break.

I was working as a second shift charge nurse at a pediatric facility in a nearby town. One of our patients had a seizure that would not let go. He had stopped breathing and was turning blue. The attendant and I worked together in clearing his airway, and he started to breathe again. What a relief! However, he still was not responding and seemed to be in a coma. I ran to the nurse's station and called the doctor for advice. While waiting on the ambulance, I administered the medication that the doctor ordered. This seemed to bring him around somewhat. His frail body continued to seize, and I was concerned that any moment he would stop breathing again. I was praying hard and trying to remain calm. I was glad to see the ambulance pull in. In a short time he was on his way to the local hospital ER.

I fell into a chair in the break room and reached for the cigarettes in my pocket. I lit one and drew deeply on it as I whispered a thank you God for sparing this child's life. There was an attendant in the room taking her break as well. When she heard me talking to myself and thanking God she asked, "Are you a Christian?" I nodded my head. "You sit there smoking and thanking God, and you call yourself a Christian?" She went on to expound on her church's doctrine. I was stunned and absolutely speechless. I looked at her, and I got up and went back to the nurse's station and started doing my charting. It hadn't been crazy enough I was thinking to myself. Now some nutty girl is attacking me personally. Who does she think she is? I didn't like her and had disliked her since we first met. I had been informed she would be working for me after school and on weekends, and she had special permission from the director of nurses to wear skirts and dresses to work. She was a Pentecostal minister's daughter. When I looked at her I knew she was one of those "holiness" people.

I went home that night and sleep didn't come easily. I was exhausted physically, mentally, emotionally, and now thanks to Robin, spiritually as well. The next morning, I woke up with her words ringing in my head once again. I had never had anyone be that outspoken, especially about religion.

I dreaded going into work that evening and facing her and didn't tell anyone about what had happened. I got the dayshift nursing report, and everyone had left the nurse's station when she came up and handed me a piece of notebook paper. She said, "I'm sorry. I know I made you very angry last night. Will you read these scriptures? They will help you understand." I took them and stuffed them in my pocket. For the rest of the night, I avoided her deciding to read the letter at home.

I took the letter out of my pocket the next morning and read it. She had written down a lot of scriptures, Acts 2:38, Mark 16:16; and, the more I read the more disturbed I became. I didn't remember ever reading these scriptures before. I put them away in a drawer, and I never spoke of them again to her or anyone else for many years.

She only worked at the facility for a few months, and I was not unhappy about that. I would on occasion think of the scriptures, what she had said, and would feel this uneasy feeling which I couldn't explain. Soon I left the facility for another job closer to home. I didn't think of her at all anymore or the scriptures. My life was busy and full with my husband, two sons, going to school part time and working full time.

I came across the scriptures again one day and put them in my purse to ask a friend what she thought about them. She expressed I had done what the Bible said to do to be saved and that these people were just "messing with my head." I stuffed them back into a pocket of my purse and forgot about them.

As time went by I realized I had this huge void in my spiritual life. I went to church regularly, but it seemed that I got little out of the services. I would sit and listen thinking to myself, "There has to be more than this." Before attending my church on Sunday morning I had started watching a TV evangelist. I loved watching this program. The music was awesome, and the people worshipped openly often raising their hands with tears running down their happy faces. I would have this longing inside to be there experiencing that kind of worship.

As given in an earlier account in time, I went to First Apostolic Church in North Vernon and received the Holy Ghost and was baptized in the name of Jesus. One of the first people I thought of when I came up out of the water was Robin. I continued to think of Robin hoping the Lord would find a way for us to reunite even though I didn't even know her last name and had not seen her for ten years. Well, the Lord found a way.

My older son had graduated from college and was traveling in his job. He asked me to take him to the airport to catch his flight. I asked my brother to ride up with us. My son asked if I would stop at a convenience store in the nearby town where I had worked as a nurse. I stopped while he ran in and back out because they didn't have the shampoo he used. Then I took him across the road to another store.

My brother and I were sitting in the car waiting for my son to come out of the store when a car pulled up beside us. I heard this peck on my window and turned around. There stood Robin! While rolling down my window she said, "Aren't you Rena Dillman, the nurse that I used to work with?" I said, "Robin, guess what? I have the Holy Ghost and I've been baptized in Jesus' name." She started jumping up and down in the parking lot, and I started crying. We had a precious reunion in just a few minutes after all those years. God had heard my prayer and answered it in a miraculous way. I was so overwhelmed by the events that had just taken place. The chance of that all unfolding without the hand of God directing it was zero to nil. He cared enough for me and for her to allow us to reconcile and to know the joy of answered prayer.

God has been so merciful. He has sent amazing, loving and nurturing people into my life to bring His Gospel. It took me years to receive it but thank God for His mercy and love. I have found Him to be faithful these past twenty years while walking together in His truth.

Special Note: After a few years I donated the purse to a charity organization. Sadly I realized after it was gone that I had not removed the scriptures that Robin had handwritten. I have a feeling they ended up in the hands of someone else who needed to hear the Acts 2:38 message. I only hope that when I get to heaven I can meet that person. All three of us will shout together and jump up and down on the streets of Glory. Halleluiah!!

Where Angels Might Fear To Tread

Many years ago I sat on a church pew praying during a moving altar call. I heard this sobbing, almost whimpering, coming from an individual on the far end of my pew. I immediately began focusing my prayer on this individual who seemed to be under great conviction. As the sobbing became louder and louder, I felt a need to at least invite them to the altar to pray. I was hesitant, but it seemed right.

I put my arm around her and asked if we should go to the altar and pray. She shook her head indicating "no" and continued to cry. I sat there for a few minutes and prayed asking God for guidance. I felt such compassion for this individual and concern. I approached again. She insisted God could never forgive her. I then tried to explain there was nothing God could not forgive; however, I felt a resistance to any words of comfort. After a few minutes, I returned to my end of the pew feeling so helpless.

Later, I inquired about this individual. I was told a story I will never forget. It changed the way I perceive people crying during a church service and the way I pray for them. This individual had lost a child in a way that had caused them a great deal of guilt and regret. I understood more clearly the anguished sobs I thought were coming from a sinner in need of salvation. How I wish I had been more spiritually wise and mature. I would have wrapped my arms around her, prayed and cried with her! I realized I had tried to go where even angels might have feared to tread.

Angels Outside My Window

It was July 15, 1988. My friend Martha Carson was in critical condition in a Louisiana hospital intensive care unit. Her life was hanging in the balance. After eighteen hours of diagnostic tests and emergency surgery, she was unrecognizably swollen from congestive heart failure due to the toxins of a ruptured colon. The doctor in charge had informed the family of the seriousness of the situation and the possibility of their losing her.

As she lay there in the hospital bed under the effects of the anesthetic and pain medication, she was acutely aware of a figure pacing back and forth in front of her room. She recognized the figure as the devil. He continuously went from a phone booth around the corner, and then back, to stand mockingly in front of her hospital room door. He held a piece of paper in his hand with the telephone number of the mortuary in the small Mississippi town where she grew up. She became aware of voices in conversation realizing they were discussing her. The voices belonged to the devil and God. After a period of time she heard God emphatically tell the devil, "You cannot kill her." She knew at that moment she was not going to die. She relaxed and drifted back into oblivion.

On that same night, I was lying in my bed in Hope, Indiana tossing and turning unable to sleep. Feeling very troubled and uneasy in my spirit, I prayed for everything and everyone that came to my mind. Eventually I felt an urgency to pray for my friends Tony and Martha Carson. I prayed for what seemed like hours, unable to fall asleep. As I prayed voices seemed to be coming from outside my closed bedroom window. The voices became louder, and I strained to hear what they were saying. Getting out of bed, I went to the window to see if I could see anyone there. I couldn't see anyone, but I could still hear the voices.

My husband had fallen asleep in the TV room down the hall. Thinking he must have left the TV or radio on, I checked to see if the voices could be coming from there; but, that was not the case. Deciding not to awaken my husband, I returned to our bedroom and climbed back into bed. The voices continued to drift through the window but were more muffled now. It was 5:00 am. Exhausted, I asked the Lord to please let me go to sleep. I finally drifted off only to be awakened in a short time by the ringing of the phone. It was my pastor calling with some bad news. Martha had become acutely ill while in revival services in Louisiana. She was in very serious condition and needed a miracle from God. Now, I had an explanation for the sleepless night and once again pleaded with God to spare Martha's life

With not much sleep, I decided to go to Sunday morning church services. I didn't mention the experiences of the night to my husband or to anyone else. When arriving at church, I overheard an elderly lady telling our pastor's wife about a sleepless night. She told of hearing voices but of being unable to understand what they were saying. She, too, had prayed all night long. After hearing their conversation, I knew it was confirmation of what had happened to me during the night.

After Martha's miraculous release from the hospital, I went to her parents' home in Potts Camp, Mississippi to help while she recuperated. While there I heard another amazing story. A young woman, who attended the church Martha's father pastored in Potts Camp, was awakened during that same night in July 1988. She fell to her knees by the side of her bed in urgent prayer. While praying, she had a vision of the devil pacing back and forth from a telephone booth in a hospital hallway to the doorway of a hospital room. In his hand he had a piece of paper with the telephone number of the local mortuary written on it.

Were the voices those of angels outside our windows?

Special Note: My friend Martha not only survived but also continues to serve God as a living testimony to the healing power of God and answered prayers of God's people. Hebrews 11:1, "Now faith is the substance of things hoped for, the evidence of things not seen."

SECTION VII

Where is that Grandmother? She still paints and teaches with the knowledge now that this is a special gift from God. She doesn't take her days for granted. She realizes how quickly the years have rolled by. Her babies are approaching middle age. Her grandchildren are no longer children but teenagers. Could it be possible her grandson is driving? She celebrates 42 years of marriage today. She still feels young, light, slim and beautiful. She can almost believe that nothing has changed, but then she looks into the mirror. She looks again. Where is she Lord?

Will You Pray For Me?

My friend, Debbie, and I had just left women's prayer at our church. We had decided to stop by a local supermarket for a few grocery items before heading home. We both filled our carts with more than we intended to buy while taking advantage of their specials. We pushed our loaded carts out into the parking lot. I was leading the way, walking a little too close to the middle of the driving lane, chatting away to my friend when she suddenly yelled, "Rena, get out of the way." I turned and saw a car coming straight at me. I pushed my cart over to the side and got over as quickly as I could saying, "Wow! That was close!"

As we reached Debbie's car, the car that had almost hit me pulled into a parking space nearby. Debbie opened her trunk, and we began unloading our groceries. A woman walked over to our car and said, "I wouldn't have hit you honey. I'm not feeling too well today and really shouldn't be out driving, but I needed a few things from the store." I told her that it was OK; I shouldn't have been so far out into the driving lane. She then shared she had a rash, a swollen face and her eyes were not working too well.

She seemingly didn't want to leave. Debbie was loading her groceries into the car as I talked to the woman. We stood there for a few seconds. Then she asked, "Will you pray for me?" I said, "We would be glad to pray. What is your name?" She told us her name, and I assured her we would pray for her on our way home. I started loading my groceries into the trunk of the car.

She apologized again for almost running me down, smiled and walked away.

We got into the car. Debbie and I just looked at each other while both stating at the same time, "Why didn't we pray for her right here in the parking lot?" She obviously had been in great need of prayer for physical healing. We agreed the reason we hadn't prayed for her on the spot was fear of what people would think or even what she would think.

We really let this woman down. After all, we had just left a women's prayer meeting. We both decided if in a similar opportunity we would PRAY! We prayed for her on the way home and prayed many times for her over the next few days.

This was a "life's little interruptions" moment that made a lasting impression. Since this experience I have tried to do better when given the opportunity to pray for others. Only God knows what we missed that day- a miracle perhaps, a new friendship or a chance to witness to her of what Jesus Christ had done in our lives. My prayer is that I will always be ready when someone asks, "Will you pray for me?"

Eight And Eighty

The summer our grandson Blake turned eight, his maternal great-grandfather turned eighty. Daddy lived with us after Mother's death, and he looked forward to the grandchildren's visits. Blake had come to spend a week like his sister Jessica did each summer. We looked forward to these special times with them individually.

Every day something special was planned, which usually included fishing (Blake enjoys fishing as much as eating). It didn't matter if they caught anything as long as he got to throw the line out into the water and sit with anticipation of the "big catch." Often the "big catch" was a little blue gill!

After a few days, Blake was looking for something a little more exciting to occupy his time. He watched movies on T.V. and played many video games. Daddy couldn't relate to these electronic toys.

Near the end of his visit Daddy said, "Come with me Blake. I'll show you how to make a real toy, like I had as a child." Blake was all excited and followed his great-grandfather out to the yard.

My curiosity got the best of me. I grabbed the camera and went out to the back porch to watch. Daddy and Blake were looking for strong but bendable branches. I was beginning to get an idea of the toy he had in mind. As soon as they found an acceptable branch, Daddy would take his pocketknife and cut it off the tree. Blake was given charge of the branches.

They finally settled down on a bench under the big maple tree in the backyard. I watched as Daddy whittled the branches down and cut slots in the ends. He went to his woodshop and got some heavy twine. In a short period of time, a bow and set of arrows had been fashioned for Blake. Daddy gave him instructions and demonstrations and related most of his toys had been handmade just like this one.

Finally after being instructed to never point at a person or animal, Blake was allowed to play freely with his new toy. He spent hours in the backyard with his homemade treasure.

As I watched those two excited white heads, one from age and the other a tow-headed youth, I thought of the many bows and arrows Daddy had made for us as kids growing up on the farm. I'm sure the same excitement was there. I'm also sure Daddy had waited with anticipation as his father had made his first bow and arrows. I could picture his light hair shining as bright as his eyes with each shot.

When it was time to leave for the trip back home, Blake did not want to part with his bow and arrows. I finally convinced him that we would hang them in the garage, and they would be there his next visit (I was just a little concerned about the image bow and arrows would conjure up). Would you believe it is still hanging in that very spot eight years later? It was never played with again. Why do I keep it? I hope that one day Blake will come across it; and, the magic of that day long ago will come rushing back. I'm sure there will be another little tow-headed boy in need of a special toy!

Short Story Forty-One

The Doily

As I look at my newly acquired treasure, I'm thinking of how it came to me. It was a special day, a good day, and a moment that will be forever indelible in my mind.

I had taken a trip to Potts Camp, Mississippi with my friend Martha. Her 89-year-old mother had been very ill with pneumonia and had been bedridden for several days. She was not bouncing back as they had hoped she would. She was tired, not responding to the cajoling of her large family. Each day they would say a few words of love and give encouragement; each night they would share events of the day and whisper prayers for the one whom they relied upon so heavily.

She started to perk up after our second day and sat in her chair and talked to us. Martha then told me to go into the front bedroom and look at the beautiful comforter that someone had made for her mother with the names of the parents and each of the ten children professionally embroidered in quilted squares. I had never seen anything like it. She asked her mother to show the antiques located in another room that had belonged to her mother's sister. With much enthusiasm, she pointed out the antique pieces as well as the mementoes of her late husband. She came across some old handkerchiefs that had been hand worked around the edges and pulled one out that had been tatted by her mother. This handkerchief was given to Martha. She then went over and pulled out a bag of doilies and asked Martha if she would like to have a white one. Her mother had also made it. Then she asked me if I had any doilies and if I would like one too. She gently pulled out a white one with rose and pink trim around the edges and gave it to me. Her mother had made it as well. What a precious gift! She turned and told us that the doilies reminded her of a dream she had had, maybe that day. Then she proceeded to tell it.

I was at a sale or auction with many boxes of things on the ground. A girl came over to one of the boxes and pointed at a beautiful doily sticking out of the edge of the box. "I want that one," she said. I reached down, and when I pulled it out all that was left of it was just a small portion or fragment of the doily. Isn't it strange I would have such a dream while we are now looking at these doilies? Martha and I looked at each other as the moment seemed to be frozen in time. I had chill bumps all over my body.

I've thought about what her dream might have meant and the connection it might have had to her giving us the doilies. Could it mean that only the small portion of her life is left? Could the last fragment of her life be the most beautiful?

When looking at my treasure, I will think of her as well as that day and that special moment in time. I will be reminded of life and its intricacy and its fragility. The last fragment could be the most beautiful. I have a strong feeling it is for her. God may have given her a small glimpse of the beauty to come, for a life well lived for Him.

The Fragrance of Christmas

As a child growing up on our Franklin County Indiana farm, Christmas was my favorite time of year. Daddy would go into the woods and cut down our tree, usually a cedar. He would place it in a five-gallon bucket filled with heavy rocks and plenty of water. Mother would place a white sheet or quilt around the bottom to hide the bucket.

Decorating the tree was always a fun time for my brothers and me, untangling the old bubble lights and picking apart the icicles that were saved from year to year. After tiring of hanging each one individually, we would finally end up throwing the icicles on the tree and each other. Many of our decorations were handmade, and we usually fussed about who would hang theirs in the front of the tree where they could be seen and admired the most. How excited we would be when the tree was all decorated and Daddy would place the star on the top. The fragrance of the cedar permeated the whole house. The fire burned brightly in the wood stove close by, and we all sat on the floor around the tree and basked in its beauty while Mother made hot cocoa with marshmallows.

Our family always had a live tree when I was growing up and for many years after I married. During my senior year in high school, I was dating my future husband. Don was invited to join us on our trek in the woods to cut down our Christmas tree. We had moved to town by this time, but it didn't keep us from our annual tradition. A farmer, who was a friend of our family, allowed us to cut any tree we wanted from his woods. The snow was deep which made our task more difficult, but we managed to cut down and bring home the most beautiful eight-foot standing fir tree. When we finished decorating it, we sat on the floor and admired our handiwork. The house, once again, smelled like Christmas.

As the years rolled by my parents went to an artificial tree. The fragrance of Christmas changed to freshly baked cookies, a turkey in the oven and a candle that was remindful of the cedar trees of my childhood. Since Christmas has always been my favorite time of the year, my tree of one became three and then five trees. Decorating for the holidays continues to be a labor of love and time well spent as I am reminded each year while admiring the beauty of each tree.

Mother became ill in 1994. The diagnosis of her illness seemed to elude the doctors, even the specialists. Her illness required frequent trips to the hospital for blood work; so, I usually fixed lunch or dinner for them before they returned home. On one of these visits around Christmas time, Mother noticed one of the small trees I had in my family room. She requested I select a tree like mine as well as ornaments for her. Mother put the small tree up that year and enjoyed it very much. We had no idea that it would be her last Christmas with us. She became acutely ill and passed away in February. Daddy came to live with us for two and one-half years before moving into his own apartment nearby.

That first Christmas without Mother was unbelievably empty. I got through it, but there was little joy in my heart or decorating that year. Later while looking at photos of Mother's last Christmas, I noticed the little tree and wondered where it might be. I thought it would be very special to put it up and decorate it in her memory.

Daddy couldn't remember where he stored it. Each year I would ask again if he had found it. I finally gave up asking after seven years.

In 2003 as I was decorating the house for the holidays, Daddy came in carrying a plastic Sears bag with what looked like Christmas ornaments in smaller bags inside. He handed me the bag. With tears in his eyes he headed back down to his house. I took the bag of ornaments and sat down in the nearest chair. I carefully untied the bag. As I did Mother's perfume filled my nostrils and the air. Tears began to flow as I sat and held the bag, cradling it in my arms. As I breathed in the fragrance of my mother, I envisioned her performing the traditional New Year's Day task of taking down the tree-of her wrapping each ornament in tissue paper and her perfume permeating them. Unknowingly, she had given me a gift that I would not receive until seven years later–The Fragrance of Christmas.

Very carefully, with love and thanksgiving spilling over in my heart, I folded the bag that had held the tree ornaments and placed it in a special box hoping to savor and preserve this precious gift forever.

Standing L. to R. Roger, Robert, Gregory, Ronald,
Rena
Seated L. to R. parents' Clifton and Nola, Randy -
taken on my parents 50th anniversary

The Brush Of An Angel's Wing

Everyone had slept in that cold blustery morning in February with the exception of Reverend Tony Carson. He had chaplain duty at a nearby Army base and had left hours earlier. When our friends, Tony and Martha Carson come to visit, we usually stay up late talking. It had been well past midnight the previous night when we finally went to bed after praying together, specifically for Don and Martha's physical healing.

The warmth of my bed was tempting me to ignore the alarm clock and drift off to sleep again. Hesitantly, I decided to get up and head for the family room. On my way to my favorite recliner, I grabbed a warm throw and then snuggled under its warmth against the cool morning temperature.

It wasn't long before Martha appeared and sat on the sofa opposite me. We talked about the good night's rest we had enjoyed. She seemed to be in deep thought. Finally she looked at me as if there was something of importance within. She told of being awakened during the night from a sound sleep by what felt like a soft feather brushing across her legs. It was not frightening or alarming. The sensation was of a soft brush against her skin. She checked to see if her husband had taken the blanket off but found him to be sleeping soundly beside her. The thought then occurred that perhaps I had come in and placed an extra blanket on their bed. She realized the door was closed, and I would have knocked before entering. "Rena, what do you think? Has anyone mentioned having a similar experience in that room?" I told her that no one had mentioned such an experience even though many people had suggested through the years how peaceful our home felt to them. As I sat and listened to this incredible story I began to have a feeling of what it might have been-the brush of an angel's wing! She readily agreed that was exactly what it felt like-an angel's feather brushing across her skin.

I noticed the mailman walking past the window and decided to go out to the mailbox. Along with the mail, I found a note and a tape from our friend David Webster. I read the note on my way back into the family room. It piqued my interest when reading the tape had two songs about angels from an upcoming CD by his sister Sally Webster, a gifted songwriter and musician. I asked Martha if she would like to hear the tape, and she eagerly agreed. We sat and listened in awe to the words of the songs that told of "an angel watching over us," and then asking the questions, "Do you feel the chill every now and then? Could it be a pair of angel wings?" It was as if we were receiving confirmation of what had happened to Martha during the night.

Later that evening over dinner we talked again of Martha's angel experience. Reverend Carson felt it had been a ministering angel since much prayer had recently gone up for her physical healing.

Special Note: I called David the next day. David then shared of how Sally had written one song after enduring a long and painful ear infection requiring surgery to resolve. After reading my manuscript for this book, he felt a tugging to deliver the tape. He and Sally have graciously given their permission to include the lyrics to the two songs on the tape placed in my mailbox at exactly the right time- another example of God's perfect timing!

May these words from Sally's heart bless you as they did us.

Angel Watchin' Over Me

There must be an angel watchin' over me
On the road to a place I don't know

There must be an angel watchin' over me
Everyday everywhere that I turn

There must be an angel watchin' over me
I feel a brush from a heavenly touch

There must be an angel watchin' over me
Til' the day when I hear them say

I must be an angel watchin' over you
On the road to a place you don't know

I must be an angel watchin' over you
Everyday everywhere that you turn

I must be an angel watchin' over you
You'll feel a brush from a heavenly touch

I must be an angel watchin' over you
Til' the day when you hear them say

You must be an angel

Pair of Wings

Chorus
There's a pair of wings that take care of me
Even when I don't know they're around
They encircle me and hold me close
Even when I'm down

Sometimes I feel a touch or just a brush
Of a feather from her wings
They encourage me to take a stand
Or make it through the day

Chorus
Oh yes they're always there every night and day
She enfolds me with her wings
Saying "Please don't fear I am always here
Protecting you always"

Chorus
Do you feel a chill every now and then
Could it be a pair of angel wings
Watching over you guarding night and day
Just for you always

Chorus
Ending
Yes there's a pair of wings Angel wings
Angel wings Angel wings

In Memory of Jerika

For many years now, Mondays have been a special time of coming together for a group of ladies, and on occasion a brave man or two, for weekly art classes. We range in age from the teenager and young adult to the older generation. Our common bond is our love of art. We share our artistic accomplishments, our joys, sorrows, our grandchildren's latest antics, our likes, dislikes, politics, religion and our current aches and pains. We laugh a lot and sometimes cry. Many tears have fallen since the tragic loss of Jerika Bair and her nephew Bryce on September 4, 2002.

Jerika brought many joys and much laughter to our group. She had a delightful giggle and a beautiful smile. She had a definite flair for the artistic. She loved the color purple with many of her paintings reflecting that love and her love of intense colors. If I walked past her while she was working and raised my eyebrows in question, she would say, "But I like that color." I'm so glad she chose the colors she liked while expressing herself on the canvas. Jerika was truly creative and was developing into a fine artist. She was also a part of the Wednesday class of church school and home school students who were her peers. There was much laughter in those classes and much paint that went home on clothing. Their parents probably wondered at times what they were painting!

Jerika was much too busy to clean her brushes with paper towels. Often she stuck them in her ponytail in order to easily grab them when needed. She would sometimes have five or more brushes in her hair sticking out in all directions. Cleaning her brushes on her clothing was a habit since it was also quicker. Many of her paintings were done with a family member or friend in mind. Her sisters, Hilary and Whitney, asked her to do a special project for their sorority. It was four huge owls sitting on a log. She talked to those owls a lot while painting them.

At Easter she wore her bunny ears to class and brought candy. At Christmas she gave each of us a handmade gift. She got a new puppy and brought it to class so she could care for it. We passed it around like a new baby. As a charter member of the Art Guild of Hope, Jerika rarely missed a meeting. She actively participated in the business meetings. I still see her bright eyes with the mention of Easter and Christmas projects on the town square, and she was always the first to eagerly sign up.

Jerika took on the task of doing our yard work. We fought the war on weeds and crab grass and planted flowers together. She did whatever odd jobs around the house that needed to be done with enthusiasm and creativity. From her loving parents and siblings, she gained an understanding of the importance of serving others and her community. She had a servant's heart and hands, always ready to put them to the task at hand. Jerika indeed bloomed wherever she was planted.

We teased her and shared our tales of woe with her. We loved her like a sister, our child and grandchild. She was one of the girls. Oh, how we will miss her. Life begins with an empty canvas. Jerika filled hers and ours with color and love.

Jerika Bair in Art class

Conclusion

As I sat and visited with a friend recently, we talked of being in the winters of our lives, of how quickly the years have gone by, and how it was hard to believe our children were approaching middle age. We admitted still feeling thirty-nine in our minds even if our bodies reminded us on a daily basis that we are not thirty-nine.

We agreed that the one good thing about growing old, actually the best thing, is being able to look back and understand the difference Jesus Christ has made in our lives.

I've been able, as I have written these stories, to pinpoint the numerous times that God has sent His angels, literally and figuratively, in the form of friends and strangers to minister in times of personal and family crisis.

Has there been fear? Oh yes, but out of that fear, faith has grown. It is a faith birthed many generations ago, nurtured, treasured and handed down through the years so the cycle could continue.

In sharing their life stories, my mother and my grandmothers passed on their legacy of faith. Within the pages of this book, I now pass them on to the next generation. I pray members of the next generation will someday write their own life stories of how faith has overpowered fear in their lives.

Now, in the winter of my life, I find comfort and warmth in my life's quilt wrapped tightly around me. Made by the many hands of loved ones and treasured friends, it envelops me with sweet memories of them. Some memories bring a smile; others bring a tear. Each brings a longing to reach out and to grasp and tightly hold on to while never wanting to let them go.

But I must let go; I must toss my quilt to the side. It is a new day that God has so graciously given to greet and to continue my journey. New pieces will be added to my quilt today, sewn by the hands of precious family members, new and old friends, strangers, perhaps angels, and the most tender and loving hands of all-the hands of God.

May God bless you on your journey,

Rena Blake Dillman

Short Story 2 – They've Come For Me

"The Old Rugged Cross" - words and music by George Bennard

Section II – What happened to that young girl?

"Jesus Loves Me" – words by Anna B. Warner; music by William B. Bradbury

Short Story 26 – Mom I Need To Talk To You

"Take Me Home, Country Roads" – words and music by John Denver

Short Story 29 – The Gift

"Thanks To Calvary" – words and music by Bill and Gloria Gaither

Short Story 43 – The Brush Of An Angel's Wing

"Angel Watchin' Over Me" – words and music by Sally Webster

"Pair of Wings" – words and music by Sally Webster

About The Author

Rena resides in Hope, Indiana with her husband Don. They are the parents of two sons and proud grandparents of two. They are both active in church and community projects. Rena is founder and current president of Art Guild of Hope. She has taught adult and children's art classes for twenty-four years and currently teaches in her studio located on the Hope town square.

Laugh,

Cry,

To Block Emotion,

Is To Block Life…

(David Webster – Family Connections)

Printed in the United States
40160LVS00001B/157-255